THE OVERSEAS CHINESE

The
Overseas Chinese

A BACKGROUND BOOK

Lois Mitchison

DUFOUR EDITIONS

CHESTER SPRINGS

PENNSYLVANIA

© The Bodley Head Ltd. 1961
Library of Congress Catalog Card number : 61-16577
Manufactured in Great Britain
First published in the U.S.A. 1961

CONTENTS

AUTHOR'S NOTE

I am most grateful to Mr. Guy Wint who very kindly read and commented on this book. He is, of course, not responsible for any errors of fact or interpretation I may have made. I am also most grateful for help and stimulating suggestions given me by Mr. Richard Harris and Mr. Derrick Sington.

L. M.

1

The Corpses' Hotel

THE favourite Sunday picnicking place for a good many Chinese families in Hong Kong is the Corpses' Hotel. It looks like an old-fashioned Chinese country house with white-washed walls, red-tiled roofs, and rooms arranged round several open courtyards. In the first courtyard there is an open summer house, the traditional 'moon-viewing pavilion', and in fine weather the custodian sometimes sets out his tray of drying jasmine tea-leaves there. He keeps his white pigeons just off the courtyard; and also, less romantically, his hens. Beyond the courtyards of the hotel the hill falls steeply to the blue-green sea scattered with the brown sails of fishing junks and small Chinese and British-held islands.

The point of the hotel is to house temporarily the bodies of the overseas Chinese who have died outside China but still want to be buried in the villages their families came from. There are generally several hundred of the solid, wide Chinese coffins waiting in the hotel, and many more boxes of bones. The bones have had to be ceremonially washed in rice wine by the dead man's relations after his body has been buried for several years in some temporary overseas cemetery. Generally there are also a few urns of ashes, but ordinary Chinese tradition is against cremation. How, the older members of the family ask, can a man eat, drink and travel in the hereafter, if his body is not with him? But sometimes (in Thailand particularly) Chinese customs clash with other burial customs. Then even Chinese, traditional enough to respect an honoured father's desire for burial in his native village, may still follow the customs of their new country rather than the customs of their race and allow cremation after a suitable preliminary burial.

In the coffins, particularly those in the hotel's expensive private rooms, there are a few embalmed bodies from the Chinese communities in Liverpool and London, and more from the much bigger Chinese 'towns' in San Francisco and the rest of America. In the big public hall the proprietor has his own small altar of a chair and table dedicated to the kitchen and household gods of Chinese tradition, and the air smells all the time of incense from the sticks burning in front of the stacked-up baskets and coffins. The dead in the hall have come from Australia, from the Pacific islands, from Peru and the Caribbean and from all over south-east Asia. 'Malaya,' said the custodian, pointing to one of the biggest piles of baskets, 'and Singapore: over there Vietnam, Laos, and Cambodia, Indonesia, Thailand, the Philippines and Burma.' He shoo-ed outside, into the courtyard, a small child from one of the picnicking families who was looking inquiringly at the red poster of the kitchen god.

To Chinese—children or adults—there is nothing odd or frightening about the Corpses' Hotel. Young men, whether they are the scientific graduates of American universities or traditionally brought-up young farmers and businessmen, find it very natural that their elders should want to be buried 'at home'—even if that home is several thousands of miles away and the elder himself has in fact never seen it. All he knows are the descriptions his father gave him, and the letters from relations left in the old family village. But on the elder's death somewhere in San Francisco, Thailand or Malaya the sons of the family will arrange for their father's local funeral, and then for his stay in Hong Kong. Meanwhile the relations in China fill in forms and negotiate with the authorities for the crossing of the frontier and the final

10

Chinese burial. Under the new government of China it is still possible for bodies to be sent over the frontier, but it takes longer than it used to do, and there are more formalities.

Once in China it is still sometimes possible for the dead to be buried in the traditional family graveyard where the graves are swept and planted with flowering trees by the women of the family. But other graveyards, in villages where the small private farms have been merged into large communes, have been ploughed up and sometimes the bodies have been moved. It is in the interests of higher agricultural production and more food for the village as a whole, the new commune officials say; but to some traditional Chinese, in and out of China, the ploughing up of the graves is the most shocking single action of the communist government.

2

The Emigrants

To some westerners the whole idea of the Corpses'
Hotel is startling; startling that death should be accepted
so readily by the Chinese families who picnic there; and
much more startling as evidence of the countries all
round the world with Chinese communities in them,
and the strength of the ties, at any rate among some of
the older members of these communities, that bind the
overseas Chinese to their ancestral homes in China and
the traditions of their people.

There are between 12 and 13 million overseas Chinese.
It is almost impossible to say exactly what the total
numbers are, or the numbers in most given countries.
Censuses in south-east Asia are not always accurate, many
Chinese and half-Chinese have good economic and social
reasons for not wanting to stress their race to government officials, and these officials may have their own
nationalist reasons for wanting to over- or under-stress
the Chinese numbers and 'the yellow peril' in their
country. Sometimes men a quarter or an eighth Chinese
still think of themselves as belonging to their great-
grandfather's race; more often they believe they are stat-
ing the whole truth when they say that they are Thais
or Indonesians.

In America there are about 120,000 known Chinese,
and there are a few thousand in the Caribbean, in Peru,
in Britain, and in Australia. But most of the overseas
Chinese are in south-east Asia. The biggest communities
are in Malaya and Singapore (with around 2,365,000
Chinese and 965,000 Chinese respectively); and in Thai-

land with between 2 and 2½ million Chinese. (But estimates of the Thai Chinese population can vary by over a million according to who is making them, and whom they count as Chinese.) In Malaya, which has a total population of 6,250,000, the Chinese are the biggest single racial community; and in Singapore, with a total population of 1,260,000, the Chinese are the majority people. In Thailand more than one person in ten is Chinese. In the three small colonies of British Borneo, with a total population of a million, one person in four is Chinese.

Elsewhere in south-east Asia the Chinese are a smaller minority. In Indonesia, the country with the region's biggest population, the 2,250,000 local Chinese mean that around one person in forty is Chinese. In South Vietnam there are about 780,000 Chinese in a total population of 12 million; in North Vietnam rather fewer Chinese in a slightly larger total population. In Laos there are 10,000 Chinese among a population of 1,750,000; in Cambodia 230,000 among 4,200,000; in the Philippines 270,000 among 22,280,000; and in Burma 320,000 among 20,300,000. Over nearly all of south-east Asia the Chinese birthrate is high, and the Chinese community increases more quickly than the local population.

Nearly all these immigrant Chinese have come from a quite small area of south China: the four provinces of Kwantung, Kwangsi, Fukien and Hainan Island. The Chinese migrant peoples are physically alike, but they speak different dialects, according to which province and which towns and villages they come from; and to some extent each dialect group has tended to emigrate to its own particular country, and to specialise in particular jobs. The biggest group of Chinese in Thailand speak Teochiu; and among the most far-flung Chinese communities in America, Australia and Britain the majority of the people are Cantonese. The Cantonese also (perhaps because they come from the area round the biggest city in the emigrant region) have often been the best artisans and engineers in the overseas Chinese communities, and provided a high proportion of the teachers and doctors; and, in recent years, the most ardent nationalists and revolutionaries. To an outsider the Cantonese are a particularly attractive people. They are quick-spoken and quick-acting, in contrast to the more rural peoples like the Hakkas. Most Chinese believe that the small, delicate Cantonese women are the most beautiful their country has, and the Cantonese tradition of cookery, particularly of small cakes and savouries, is said to be one of the most elaborate in China.

* * *

The first Chinese to visit most of south-east Asia were traders sailing in ships built and manned from south China. At the end of the 13th century, when the Chinese foreign trade was well established, Marco Polo described the fleet that took him to India and Persia. The ships had about sixty small cabins 'each of them affording accommodation to one merchant' and their holds were divided into thirteen watertight bulkheads. This, according to Marco Polo, was because of whales. 'For, when sailing at night, the motion through the waves causes a white foam that attracts the notice of the hungry animal. In expectation of meeting with food it rushes violently to the spot, strikes the ship, and often forces in some part of the bottom.... The crew, upon discovering the situation of the leak, immediately remove the goods from the division affected by the water, which in consequence of the boards being so well fitted, cannot pass from one division to another.'

Shortly after Marco Polo's time a Portuguese describes the goods carried to the Malay port of Malacca by four-masted Chinese junks. They had cargoes, he writes, of sugar, fine raw silk, porcelain, damasks, brocades and satins, musk and rhubarb, silver and pearls, gilded coffers, fans and other baubles. From Malacca the Chinese ships took pepper, incense, saffron, coral (shaped and unshaped), vermilion, quicksilver, opium and drugs. All over south-east Asia the trade pattern was the exchange of Chinese manufactured goods, particularly cloth and porcelain, Chinese medicines and specialised Chinese crops against local spices, drugs and sometimes metals.

As well as trading, Chinese fleets were sometimes charged with maintaining the vague overlordship of most of south-east Asia that the Emperor's court claimed. Local kings were particularly ready to accept Peking's supremacy when they wanted imperial confirmation of their titles against local rivals. Moreover the tribute missions that in return they occasionally sent to China were often scarcely disguised and very profitable trade missions bringing back valuable Chinese 'presents' to their countries.

The first Chinese to settle in south-east Asia were often ships' crews who stayed, with or without imperial permission, to rebuild their junks in cheap, local wood, or to take advantage of particularly favourable trading conditions and local demands for Chinese skills. But by the 18th and 19th centuries political disorder and overcrowding in the villages of south China were driving adventurous men, without past experience of the sea, out of their homes. Most southern family farms were less large than a good-sized English field, famine followed one year's bad crops, and villages fought each other for unclaimed land.

Politically there was constant trouble in the south. Bandits and pirates flourished, and villages, at any rate in the more recent decades, suffered at least equally from the looting of legitimate, but unpaid, armies. The last resistance to the 17th-century conquest of China by the Manchus was in the south, and the adherents of the fallen Ming dynasty had either to emigrate or join the local bandits.

In the 19th century it was the south that suffered particularly from the Opium War and the other western attempts to open up China, and especially the geographically convenient south Chinese ports, to foreign trade. Because of local distress the south provided many recruits to the 19th-century Taiping rebellion, with its background of peasant grievances and half-understood Christianity; and the families of the rebels, faced with savage imperial reprisals, escaped when they could, either to the emigrant ships or into banditry.

In the early part of this century the south, particularly Dr. Sun Yat-sen's own city of Canton, had become the centre of early nationalist risings and plots. Even after the First World War south Chinese, still driven by the famine, banditry and civil wars the Nationalist governments had been unable to suppress, continued to emigrate when they could. Emigration stopped only after the communists had firmly established their new government in the south in the early 1950s.

It was easier for southerners to think of emigration overseas as a solution for their difficulties because their ancestors had themselves emigrated within historic memory from central and northern China. Southern Chinese, by the standards of other nations, are intensely home-loving. 'Being away from home one *li* is not so good as being at home,' says a traditional Chinese proverb. But they did not share the northerner's feeling that emigration is against nature. By the 19th century southern villagers increasingly expected that able young men should add to family and village fortunes by at least a period overseas.

In the 1920s an American researcher found that

Teochiu villagers called the young emigrants 'galloping guests' while stay-at-homes were known insultingly as 'ricepot-keeping turtles'. Successful emigrants sent money home both to support their own family and for village good works like schools and new roads. Sometimes money was sent to be distributed to all villagers as a holiday gift; or sometimes as a gift to those villagers who, even if they were not relations, had the same surname as the emigrant's family.

* * *

When the emigrant young men could, they scraped together the few shillings needed for their passages on one of the overcrowded emigrant ships which were likened in the 19th century to African slavers. Sometimes the boats ran out of drinking water and food on the journey, and for most emigrants a coffin-shaped space between other bunks or a small square on deck was all the shiproom they had for themselves and the bundle of luggage they took with them to their new lives.

The emigrant ships in which conditions were worst were those carrying penniless labourers recruited by Chinese coolie brokers in what was known as 'the pig trade'. Sometimes the labourers were genuine would-be emigrants who were ready to sell themselves into virtual slavery for a term of years to employers who paid their passage money. Sometimes Chinese without any wish to emigrate were kidnapped by the brokers and sold in San Francisco, Hawaii, Australia and south-east Asia. The tin miners of Malaya and the rubber and tobacco planters in Malaya and in Sumatra were particularly eager for all the labour the brokers could ship to them.

In south China during the mid-19th century several kidnapping brokers were executed, and the headquarters of the pig trade moved to Macao where the surviving brokers did better than ever. Efforts by the immigration authorities in the receiving countries to stamp out the trade met with scarcely better success until the beginning of the 20th century. There are still old men, some of them now the heads of prosperous overseas Chinese families, who describe their kidnapping fifty years ago: their journey from China in ships where sometimes half the emigrants died, and their first work overseas when they lived half-starved, and bullied by their employers, in grossly overcrowded and disease-ridden 'coolie lines'.

Another feature of the pig trade, which made it at least as unpopular among emigrants to south-east Asia as the conditions of the passage and the coolie lines, was that indentured labourers generally had to work in the more remote country areas. Most ambitious young Chinese preferred to try for work in the towns, particularly those where they had relations or at least men from the same village already established. Apart from home ties, relations and friends could give them a start in new businesses or the opportunity to train as artisans.

Even for those without fortunate connections, work as general coolies, dock labourers and rickshaw pullers in the south-east Asian towns meant higher wages and more certain employment than the same work in the south China ports. But the opening many young men preferred was as an assistant in a shop, from which they could progress to their own market stall, their small permanent shop and perhaps their own import and export business. Or an ambitious man might try to find casual work with established craftsmen—a carpenter, a mechanic or a rice mill engineer—and gradually learn a new skill. To begin with very few of the emigrants were educated, but there was always a handful of Chinese doctors, and in later years a growing number of teachers and clerks.

By the 20th century most south-east Asian towns had become dependent on their large colonies of Chinese shopkeepers and artisans. About a third of the total number of South Vietnam's Chinese live in Cholon, the enormous Chinese suburb of the capital city of Saigon, and more than half the town-dwellers of Malaya are Chinese. About the Chinese of Bangkok an Englishman commented, facetiously, after his visit there in 1911: 'One's first desire (on arriving) is to see the Siamese people, and one's last regret on leaving is that of not having found them.'

Outside the towns Chinese settled in most large villages and sometimes at important cross-roads as shopkeepers and, nowadays, as the local car mechanics. Some Chinese families lived in boats and from them bought and sold the rice crop grown by Thai and Indochinese farmers. In Borneo the Chinese boatmen moved, buying and selling, among the headhunting Dyak tribes years before they were officially 'pacified'. In mining, and on road and railway building projects, contractors offered good wages to Chinese, who were known as reliable and hardworking labourers.

For most of the immigrants, even if they had been farmers in China, farming was a second-best choice. It was partly because in most south-east Asian countries there were restrictions on the ownership of land by non-native people, and partly because of the slow returns on his labour and capital a farmer might expect compared to a tradesman. Rice farming, particularly, the main occupation of most of the local peoples, offered certain subsistence but little profit, and attracted very few Chinese. But in Malaya, even before the Chinese were officially allowed to own land there, half the Chinese immigrants settled as farmers, growing specialised and potentially very profitable crops like pineapple and rubber. They were crops that needed more constant work from the farmer and his family than most Malays were prepared to give.

Whatever they chose to do, a high proportion of the Chinese immigrants prospered. But the qualities which helped their rise did not endear them to the people among whom they were living. Many south-east Asians, particularly in the Buddhist countries of Burma, Thailand, Cambodia and Laos, have said how alien they find the Chinese immigrant's view of life. He overvalues money, they find, and undervalues leisure, religion and human relations. They are astonished at the hours the Chinese are prepared to work and at the low standard of living they put up with while they save for their families in China or to open up new opportunities for themselves.

Successful Chinese boasted that all through their lives they had started work at five in the morning, finished at ten at night, and taken no holiday except, perhaps, for three days at the Chinese New Year. In Bangkok a self-made Chinese merchant greeted Dr. William Skinner, who was studying the local Chinese community, with a blighting opening gambit: 'If you haven't come to help me make money, then I won't talk to you.'

3

Welcome followed by suspicion

To begin with, most of the south-east Asian governments were glad to see the Chinese. Ma Huan and Fei Hsin, leading members of a Ming maritime expedition, described between them the kind of welcome a Chinese man in those days might expect from a Siamese woman. 'She (the Siamese woman) is greatly pleased with him,' Fei Hsin writes, 'and will invariably prepare wine to entertain and show respect to him, merrily singing and keeping him overnight.' The husband, according to Ma Huan, was only pleased that his wife should be beautiful enough to attract a Chinese.

Less extravagant welcomes awaited later Chinese traders and immigrants. But in Thailand, the most tolerant of the south-east Asian countries, Chinese immigrants became counsellors to the kings and provincial governors. In the 18th century, Taksin, the son of a Chinese father and a Thai mother, ruled Thailand for over fourteen years. Later half-Thai and half-Chinese women became the queens and concubines of Thai kings; and the present Thai royal family, like most of the heredity nobility, can claim several Chinese ancestors.

In the colonial countries most governments found that the Chinese, as well as being reliable workers, made useful buffers between themselves and the local people. They knew local conditions, but they were not unduly sympathetic to peasant or nationalist grievances. In

Indonesia and Indochina, immigration was officially encouraged. In the Philippines the Spanish government was always nervous about Peking's possible imperial ambitions, and the raids of rebels and pirates from south China, just across the seas. But even here periods of deportations and restricted immigration alternated with the re-discovery by each new generation of officials that the islands could not do without the Chinese, and a new group of them must be admitted.

Nevertheless the early history of both the Philippines and the Dutch East Indies was marred by riots of the Chinese against what they saw as oppression by the colonialists, and retaliatory massacres of the Chinese by the Europeans. The worst of several battles in the Philippines was around Manila on St. Francis Day in 1603, when 23,000 Chinese were said to have been killed. In Java in 1740 the Dutch threatened to send as slaves to Ceylon any Chinese they found in Batavia who was unable to prove that he was making an honest living. There were riots, Dutch forts were attacked and several thousand Chinese were killed.

What happened both in Batavia and in Manila was that local jealousies and local fears of the Chinese contradicted the best interests and the general policy of the governments and the Dutch East India Company. Local Dutch and Spanish officials yielded to pressure from their compatriots and, at any rate in the case of most Dutch officials implicated in the killing of the Chinese, were afterwards punished by their home governments. During the 19th century, officially friendly government policies towards the Chinese were not interrupted by riots and massacres on the earlier Javan or Filipino scale, but local European merchants were still jealous of Chinese trading successes and commented maliciously on how these were achieved.

By the end of the First World War there was no longer

the same fear of Peking's imperialist, warlike intentions to trigger off violent reprisals against the local Chinese communities. But the officially friendly attitudes were changing. Colonial governments began to consider themselves responsible for the welfare of colonial populations, as well as the maintenance of law and order and good conditions for European trade. Officials queried the earlier policy of encouraging Chinese immigration, not because they were thinking primarily of the Chinese as rivals of European merchants, but because it was said that the Chinese restricted the economic opportunities open to the local peoples, and local peasants were exploited by Chinese moneylenders and shopkeepers. The new 20th-century American government of the Philippines placed severe restrictions on Chinese immigration.

In Malaya the first quota on Chinese male immigrants was imposed in 1933, and the first quota on Chinese women in 1938. In the small colony of British North Borneo the past encouragement of immigrant Chinese farmers, which had included free passage for the relations and friends of Chinese freeholders, stopped in the 1930s.

Most of the new generation of local south-east Asian nationalists were even more jealous and more frightened of the Chinese than the European merchants and the colonial governments. As the parties of these nationalists increased their powers, and finally took over in one south-east Asian country after another, restrictions multiplied on Chinese immigration and the rôle Chinese already in the country could play in the national life and national economies. Even in Thailand anti-Chinese feelings grew after the First World War. The first Thais to study abroad and in the new mission schools in Thailand brought back exclusive western-style nationalism, and the western stories of the growing 'yellow peril' to the independent nations of both the east and the west. In 1914 a theoretically anonymous and fiercely worded pamphlet, 'The Jews of the East', was published in Thailand, and strongly rumoured to have been written by the young King Wachirawut (Rama VIth).

The King's comparison between the Jews and the Chinese was to be made again and again. They were both minority peoples living in foreign countries that did not always welcome them. Both peoples excelled in trade, both had their own culture which they were anxious to preserve, and both peoples often had stronger loyalties to their family and race than to the countries in which they had settled.

King Wachirawut's pamphlet pictured the local Chinese as the greatest menace facing Thailand. It accused them of worshipping Mammon, and being ready to lie, rob, cheat, embezzle and kill in the pursuit of money. They were aliens, the pamphlet said, owing to their allegiance to a foreign government, and unassimilable by the countries where they lived. The Chinese were accused of being parasites on the Thai economy, buying little that was produced in Thailand, and draining off wealth from the country to send home as remittances to their families in China.

Other governors and nationalists in south-east Asian countries were equally bitter about the rôle the Chinese played in local economies. It was said that the Chinese control of commerce and industry meant that Chinese businessmen, acting together, could ruin a country, and that the natives of a country could not compete against Chinese skill in business combined with the Chinese low standard of living. In a debate in the United States senate in 1902 on the usefulness of Chinese labour in the Philippines Governor Taft echoed much local sentiment when he said: 'The Chinaman comes into this country and labours, say, for 12 silver dollars a month. Out of that, the local saying is, he saves $16 to $18. At any rate he is not there for more than three to four months before he has capital to set up a store, and when he sets up a store the Filipino who has the store next to him is driven out of business.'

Other critics alleged that Chinese businesses were exclusive, with no place in them for native assistants and apprentices, that the local peasantry were ruined by Chinese rice traders and moneylenders, and local officials were bribed by Chinese breaking local regulations or smuggling.

There was some truth in these allegations. What startled many Thai out of their traditional tolerance of the Chinese in their country was the 1910 strike in Bangkok, when the Chinese societies forced a shut-down for three to five days of all Chinese businesses. They were protesting against the Thai government's order that the local Chinese, like the Thai themselves, were to pay an annual tax. During the strike the price of rice rocketed, but what enabled Bangkok life to go on was that the street-car and power-plant employees as well as some food sellers were Thai. Thais drew the moral that the more native businessmen there were the safer the country was against another strike. But in 1958 the Chinese still controlled around 80 per cent of the Thai economy, and similarly in most other south-east Asian countries a high percentage of trade and industry was, at any rate until very recently, Chinese controlled.

In Burma, Singapore and Malaya Indian immigrants competed successfully with Chinese businessmen, and shared their unpopularity. In some of the non-Moslem countries, particularly Burma and Thailand, local women kept certain traditional forms of small shop-keeping for themselves. But Malays, in Malaya, Indonesia, or in the Philippines, never rivalled Chinese traders. Only in Sarawak, where a dying Malay aristocracy deplores the times that are against them, the more vigorous Dyaks from the interior occasionally set up their own businesses, and in a handful of cases do better than local Chinese shopkeepers.

It is an old complaint that Chinese skills strangle native skills. As early as the beginning of the 17th century, Spanish writers were lamenting that because of Chinese farming methods and Chinese imported cloth the Filipinos had forgotten how to rear fowls and flocks, how to grow cotton, and how to weave clothes. Today old handicrafts in south-east Asia are mostly dying. Everyday clothes are made of Chinese or Japanese produced cotton goods, although the expensive and beautiful local-made cloths are often still kept for festivals. Few of the local people have learnt the new mechanical skills: they complain that the only place they can conveniently learn these skills is in Chinese workshops, and the Chinese will not teach them.

For choice very few Chinese businesses will employ unrelated local people. But these small Chinese businesses seldom employ unrelated Chinese, particularly Chinese from a different language group, both because it is a Chinese tradition to employ family and clan members first, and because it is easier to work with people speaking the same language.

It is also true that the people who do most of the bribing of officials in south-east Asia are Chinese. As businessmen they are particularly hindered by red tape and theoretically well-meaning, but impracticable regulations put out by new and inexperienced governments. From Sumatra, at one time, more rubber was smuggled, mostly through Chinese hands, than left the country legally. Chinese rubber smugglers blamed inefficient government attempts to control the trade and take too big a cut of the rubber profits.

Similarly many Chinese merchants in Djakarta said they were forced into black market currency operations by the Indonesian government's attempt to maintain the legal exchange rate for the rupiah at four or five times what it was worth on the Singapore market. Everywhere in south-east Asia businessmen said that illegal methods used by some merchants, and not stopped by the government, forced all their competitors to use similar methods. In the Philippines in 1947 the executive secretary of the Chinese Chamber of Commerce commented succinctly that it took two to accomplish bribery. The Filipino official had to accept the Chinese merchant's bribe!

One set of often-repeated accusations—that the Chinese are usurers and exploiters of debt-ridden farmers—has been shown by recent research not to be the whole truth. In contrast to Indian moneylenders the Chinese, if they lend money at all, lend at what is a locally reasonable rate of interest. Most Chinese moneylenders prefer to have their loan repaid rather than to go on collecting interest for many years, and they seldom foreclose on land.

In most south-east Asian countries the amount the Chinese send home in remittances can be directly balanced against the taxes they pay, the government licences they buy and, in the past, the fees paid to governments (like those of Thailand and Malaya in the early years of British rule) by the farmers of opium and gambling monopolies—both Chinese rather than local vices. South-east Asian peoples, however, owe much more to Chinese skills than to the money directly paid by the Chinese to their local governments. Without Chinese traders, artisans and farmers in south-east Asia today modern services would be impossible to maintain—there would be no dry cleaning or car repairing in most cities for instance—and national economies would be seriously damaged by the scarcity of experienced importers and exporters. In general the Chinese are a law-abiding and hardworking section of the south-east Asian population. Governments considering new measures discriminating against them must balance the economic benefits they bring to the countries they settle in against any hindrance they may be to the development of locally staffed industries.

4

A separate Chinese society

WHETHER discrimination against the Chinese and fear of their economic power is justified depends largely on where their ultimate loyalties lie. Is the author of 'The Jews of the East' right when he writes of the Chinese as loyal only to China however long they may have lived in their host country? Or are Chinese immigrants, or at any rate their sons and grandsons, good citizens of the country of their birth? Do Chinese become real Indonesians, Malayans, Vietnamese or Thais with perhaps trifling differences in their physical appearance and a handful of different social customs?

One of the difficulties about deciding how far the Chinese have been assimilated in their host countries is that a number of different factors are involved. Physical assimilation of looks and body structure, social assimilation, political and economic assimilation may all be completed at different times. Again, any discussion of assimilation is likely to rouse strong feelings. Assimilation of, or by, an alien people is distasteful to the citizens of most countries. Even among the emotional securities of Britain, suggestions that we are being culturally or socially assimilated by the Americans, or that we in our turn are assimilating our West Indian or African immigrants, rouse individuals to fury, and newspapers to print articles suggesting government-sponsored remedies. There is talk about 'bad blood', 'bad customs', dilution of the essential 'Britishness' of Britain. Indonesians,

Vietnamese and Thais are rather more tolerant in these ways than we are, but they still have some prejudices.

For a Chinese of any education the idea of stopping being Chinese, or of his descendants doing so, is rather worse than for a Frenchman to stop being French, much worse than for a Britain, with centuries of emigration behind him, to stop being British. The Chinese is conscious that he is the heir of thousands of years of history, tradition and social refinement. He knows that when the west was lived in by a handful of cavemen China was an ordered empire. Like the Frenchman he believes not only in the past superiority of his country but also in its present superiority. To many Chinese China is still 'the middle kingdom', the centre of the world, with outside it only the barbarians: Chinese food is best, Chinese looks are best, Chinese social customs are best. Added to all this for a traditional Chinese is his conviction that his life after death depends on the continuation of his Chinese family, and on his male descendants regularly worshipping his tablets in the family's ancestral hall. It needs little foresight to see that a grandson, successfully assimilated to Thailand, Malaya or Indonesia, is unlikely to give this worship.

On the other hand the people among whom the Chinese immigrant has settled are uneasily aware that he often looks on them as his inferiors. Most Asians at least have black hair, and so are somewhat better than the red-haired, blue-eyed, and big-nosed western barbarians. But even other Asians are, many Chinese think, cultural inferiors, and physically and socially slightly obnoxious.

Many south-east Asians also find it difficult to separate one sort of assimilation and one sort of loyalty from another. They point sometimes to the persistence of certain Chinese social customs among the immigrants as signs of their political and economic loyalty to China.

Local Chinese communities certainly organise themselves into Chinese societies—although they are Chinese societies of a rather odd sort. Out-dated social customs linger on among the south-east Asian communities a generation after they have gone in China itself. It is partly loyalty to the memory of 'the old country': a memory that is based on social conditions when the immigrant as a very young man left his Chinese home; and partly insulation from political and other changes affecting social and religious life in China itself. In small communities, too, the conservative child has an advantage over his more rebellious brothers that he lacks in larger groups. In small towns one or two Chinese families will probably control all the local openings for young people. There is naturally a tendency to make the most 'filial', the most docile and the most traditionally Chinese son the heir to the family business. The rebellious son is often in rebellion because he is partly assimilated to the ways of the country of his birth. But, even if he can leave for a big town, his race may stop him finding work among the native local people, and he may find it difficult to be accepted into the close-knit Chinese business community without recommendations from his older relations.

* * *

Over the last fifteen years the contrast betwen the new communist society in China itself and the old-fashioned Chinese society of south-east Asia has been particularly marked. The old-fashioned large family, which started to break up in China with women's emancipation, is still the main social unit in most of the south-east Asian immigrant communities. Among the particularly traditional Chinese communities in North Borneo, old women, hobbling on their bound 'lily' feet, still dominate their daughters-in-law, children bow daily to their elders, and for young people marriages are arranged by the

31

family. In Singapore, among more modern families, the couple are generally allowed to meet in the tea lounge of a large hotel to see each other before the engagement is announced. After the formal engagement they may take drives together sitting in the front seat of a car, while the girl's mother and aunts or sisters sit in the back.

Immigrants' homes in south-east Asia, if the family can afford it, are built on the traditional Chinese pattern with a separate courtyard and rooms for each son and his wife. In the central hall the men of the family burn incense before the ancestral tablets, and their wives arrange paper flowers in cut-glass vases before the stiffly posed, colour-tinted photographs of the more recently dead. Asked about their religion most ordinary Chinese will say that it is 'Chinese'. Most south-east Asian temples, like country temples in China, are a curious jumble, according to one Singapore observer, of 'Buddhist idols, Taoist heroes, and fairies, and Confucian maxims'. The more educated town Chinese are generally atheist or agnostic like their contemporaries in China. But they continue to celebrate the traditional Chinese festivals. 'We have to for the servants and children,' explained one Singapore university teacher.

Singapore is almost wholly a Chinese town; but in most other south-east Asian cities the Chinese of the first and second generation also live together in their commercial centres. These centres are modelled as closely as the Chinese can get to the south China ports of twenty years ago. The streets themselves are dirty but there are poles of clean washing stuck from the upstairs windows of houses. Instead of the compulsory public cleanliness of most of today's Chinese in China, ordinary Chinese in south-east Asia throw their litter on the streets and spit and urinate publicly, but even the poorest are scrupulously clean about their persons, with morning-washed, white singlets and well-ironed khaki shorts on

32

most of the men. Westerners, to many Chinese, smell abominably.

All over south-east Asia shops with window displays of plucked, red-lacquered ducks sell Cantonese food and rice wine. The wine is served warm in teapots, and tastes, to the uninitiated, like particularly nasty sherry. Other shops specialise in the paper goods needed for funerals: paper money for the dead man to spend and paper bicycles or motor cars for him to drive in. Old men carry grass cages of fighting crickets through the streets, and boast to their acquaintances about their animals' ferocity, and the number of bets their best cricket has won fighting for his owner against inferior animals. Working-class women dressed in large straw hats and shiny black cotton tunics and trousers bargain shrilly with the stall-keepers. The young Chinese typists and girl students wear high heels and silk *cheongsams*—the tight Chinese tunic. Around the streets there is generally a faint, cinnamon-toast smell of opium, even in countries where opium smoking is strictly illegal. It is one of the most treasured—even when officially deplored—of Chinese relaxations: the equivalent to many of the English pint at a pub on a Saturday evening.

*   *   *

In their community organisations the overseas Chinese have again carried with them the traditions of a past China. Thirty years ago there were no state maternity or funeral benefits in mainland China, and far too few public hospitals, sanatoria, schools or clubs. But it was always a tradition that what the state did not provide should be given by private money. The wealthy and public-spirited Chinese businessman paid very little tax, but he was expected to contribute to his clan associations and to charitable societies. This tradition has been carried overseas. Every community has its own hospitals and schools maintained largely by private donations. Clan associations of families with the same surname or men from the same village will often pay the funeral expenses of needy members (this is one of the major expenses in a Chinese life), and associations for all the members of a Chinese speech group—Hakka, Cantonese or Teochiu—will often run their own local club-house.

The Chinese communities particularly need these sorts of institutions in south-east Asia, because even today very few south-east Asian countries offer adequate welfare facilities to their own nationals, and certainly not to immigrant Chinese. Sometimes, where Chinese form the majority of the town labouring population, local governments have used their foreignness as an explicit or an implicit excuse not to bother about welfare facilities or good labouring conditions. More often south-east Asian governments have not had the public money to provide hospitals and clubs as alternatives to those of the Chinese associations.

A less acceptable importation from old China have been the secret societies that now terrorise many overseas Chinese communities. The most notorious are the Triad, 'the heaven and earth' societies, originally started in the 17th and 18th centuries by Jacobite Chinese adhering to the old native dynasty against the Manchus. Their slogan —'overthrow the Ching, restore the Ming'—is still the avowed aim of the modern societies.

In Singapore, before the recent government clamp-down on the secret societies, the Triad had about 10,000 members. They were sworn in at elaborate initiation ceremonies which included a symbolic journey through 'the city of willows', and the initiates drinking a bowl of blood—their own, their fellow members' and a cock's mixed together. The blood was balanced on the edge of a knife to remind the new member of the death that awaited him if he betrayed the society's secrets. Most of

34

the society's funds came from 'protection' money paid by Chinese shopkeepers and businessmen. Those who refused to pay, enemies of the society or members of a rival society were knifed; or they were warned of the powerlessness of the police to protect them when bombs, home-made from electric light bulbs filled with acid, were thrown at them.

Good and bad—this Chinese society ties those who are fully immersed in it very strongly to the idea of China and being Chinese. It is not necessarily a political or an economic tie, and it is a tie to the China of the past rather than to present-day Communist China. But living in this society does separate its members from the society of the native people around them. It is a barrier to complete assimilation of one sort. But a hopeful and obvious comparison is with the immigrant European communities in the United States who carefully preserved their own social customs and religious ideas even while most of them were prepared to offer full political and economic loyalty to their new country.

5

Pre-war assimilation in the different countries

In the United States by the third generation the descendants of most European immigrants are indistinguishable from the mass of the American people. Twenty years ago this was also true for many descendants of the immigrant Chinese living in south-east Asia. The grandsons and great-grandsons of the original immigrants moved out of the completely Chinese quarters, dropped or modified many Chinese customs and often had become physically indistinguishable from local people.

What had helped particularly was the shortage of Chinese women. Until the 1920s and 1930s most Chinese families in south China stopped wives emigrating with their husbands, particularly if the husbands were not sure of their prospects in their new countries. It was supposed that the wife's presence in the home village meant that the young man must eventually return to China, and before he returned he would send regular remittances home to support his family. The best-liked pattern, from the Chinese family's point of view, was for the young man to marry before he left home, leave his wife pregnant with his first son, perhaps return temporarily to beget other children on short holidays and then return for good with his fortune made after ten or twenty years, and settle down to an honoured old age in his native place.

But the pattern did not always work out like this in practice. Many young men, from families who could not afford wedding expenses, emigrated unmarried. Others looked for a temporary or a second wife in their new countries. Those who did not make the fortunes they had looked forward to often preferred to settle with their new families in south-east Asia, rather than to return in semi-disgrace to China. Others who did make fortunes were sometimes too fond of their new families to expose them to scorn as foreign barbarians in their old Chinese households.

A second factor that helped assimilation was that the Chinese emigrants came mostly from the uneducated classes in China, and only a handful of them in the 19th century could read enough of the complicated Chinese characters to let them follow a Chinese book or newspapers. They also came from a traditionally despised area. Southerners knew that many northerners, particularly Peking men, looked down on them as too small and delicate. Southern men, said northerners, came from an uncultured region without good architecture or beautiful gardens—hardly Chinese at all—just the place to provide immigrants to barbarian countries. This meant that the despised southern peasant with no public position or esteem and no scholarly background to bind him to his country was readier than a northern scholar would have been to accept the customs of a new country.

* * *

Even under these conditions the amount of assimilation there was, and its speed, varied from country to country in the region. In Thailand, the country where assimilation was generally most complete, it took around three generations. The grandson of the original immigrant was only a quarter Chinese if both his father and his grandfather had married Thai women. He generally had a Thai name, spoke Thai for preference and Chinese only haltingly, and had probably served the traditional apprenticeship in a Thai Buddhist temple. When he died he wanted to be cremated in Thai fashion, not buried as the Chinese are. For women in Thailand assimilation often took one generation less. The half-Chinese daughters of Thai mothers copied their mothers' way of dressing their hair, their mothers' clothes and their mothers' speech and customs. In Burma, where assimilation was almost equally fast, the sons of Chinese fathers and Burmese mothers officially took their fathers' nationality, the daughters their mothers'.

Chinese assimilation in Thailand was helped by Thai willingness to accept the half- and quarter-Chinese as Thais; by the physical mixture of peoples, particularly in the southern provinces, that meant that by the end of the 19th century it was impossible to tell from a man's face and build whether he was Chinese or Thai; and by the popularity of Chinese husbands among Thai women. The Chinese were known to be better providers than Thai husbands. Thai women, many of them traders in their own right, inherited a tradition of more work for women than for men, and found Chinese qualities of industry and thrift more sympathetic than their menfolk did. In return, half-Chinese girls were eagerly sought after by Thai men because of their fair complexions, and the good wifely qualities they were supposed to possess. Traditionally a Chinese had always been able to pass as a Thai by accepting a Thai patron and Thai liability to unpaid public work, and by shaving off his queue and adopting Thai clothes. The Nationality Act of 1913–14 legalised the tradition by recognising every person born on Thai soil as a Thai.

Dr. William Skinner in his book *Chinese Society in Thailand* has suggested that assimilation was helped by the firm division between Chinese and Thai society. This was symbolised by the need for a Chinese, when he decided to become a Thai, to adopt different clothes

and a different way of wearing his hair. It stopped second-
and third-generation Chinese drifting into a half-Chinese,
half-Thai society which would have been far more durable under south-east Asian conditions than a completely
Chinese society.

*　　*　　*

This half-and-half society was what grew up, and did
prove very durable in both Indonesia and Malaya. Here
the Moslem religion of the Malays, in Malaya and Indonesia, made complete assimilation more difficult. Moslem
women, even if they sometimes did so, were not supposed
to marry non-Moslem Chinese. Pork, the favourite holiday dish of the Chinese, is forbidden to Moslems. The
Koran lays down a number of social rules—ways to wash,
eat and live—many of which were contrary to Chinese
custom.

Most Malays are however not such strictly orthodox
Moslems as to make assimilation impossible on that head
alone. But Malaya and Indonesia were also colonial
countries. The colonial powers discouraged Chinese
assimilation. The Chinese were given privileges, notably
special legal rights in Indonesia, and recognised by the
British and the Dutch as separate communities whose
members, on the whole, ranked above local people. Moreover the Chinese immigrants were nearly all ambitious
—otherwise they would not have been immigrants. They
saw that the top ranks of colonial European society were
closed to them, and successful self-made men and their
descendants had no desire to join the native people and
apparently lower themselves.

What grew up was the Peranakan Chinese society in
Indonesia and the Baba Malayan Chinese society of the
old ports of Malacca and Penang. The half-Chinese, half-
Malay families married within themselves, spoke their
own dialect—a mixture of the two languages with Malay

predominating particularly among the later generations —and wore clothes that were a compromise between Malay and Chinese fashions. Chinese admirals who had visited local ports, and local Chinese heroes, were worshipped as minor deities, together sometimes with Malay princes who were traditionally supposed to have helped their Chinese subjects. By the end of the 19th century these societies had more than three hundred years of tradition behind them. Old homes in Djakarta and along the water's edge in Malacca are still beautifully furnished with a collection of heirlooms—part Chinese and part Malay. There is generally a central hall for ancestral worship, shown to visitors by its owner in something of the same spirit as an English squire shows off his family portrait gallery. The household food, in most cases, is highly spiced and oily—in the Malay tradition rather than the Chinese. But the householder and his family still call themselves Chinese, take some pride in Chinese achievements, particularly local Chinese achievements, and often contribute to local Chinese schools and hospitals.

* * *

In Indochina, as in Indonesia and Malaya, the Chinese generally considered themselves superior to the local people. In return for the 19th-century recognition by China of the French protectorate over the area, the French agreed to allow the Chinese of Indochina a privileged legal position and special tax exemptions. All the same the peoples of Indochina are not Moslems, and the Buddhists of Laos and Cambodia were as tolerant of the Chinese as their co-religionists in Thailand and Burma, and as ready to intermarry with them.

In Vietnam most observers find it impossible to tell a south Chinese, on his first appearance, from a North Vietnamese. The first Chinese settlers arrived in Vietnam more than 2,000 years ago, and for several hundred years Vietnam has been administered by Chinese as an integral part of China. The two countries share many of the same social customs, the same ideas on buildings and cooking, and a joint historical tradition of an all-powerful emperor with a mandarin civil service under him recruited by examination. But, at most periods, there was less intermarriage than in Thailand or even in the Philippines. Helped by their special privileges the Chinese immigrants into Vietnam did not generally take long to establish themselves financially, and travel to Vietnam from south China was easy. Chinese women joined their husbands there, early in the 20th century and in the 19th century, far more often than they ventured to the more remote Chinese communities.

For their part the Vietnamese learnt to distrust and fear the Chinese. In their history most of the heroes and heroines had led Vietnamese resistance against invading Chinese armies. One of the best known of the North Vietnamese groups of legends centred round a poor farmer's son: Le Loi. At the beginning of the 15th century the Chinese armies occupied the country, and the leaders of Vietnamese resistance were led to Le Loi by mystical signs. But Le Loi would not accept the leadership of his people until one day his plough turned up a golden emperor's seal. Then he travelled to Hanoi, and threw his fishing nets into the lake in the centre of the town. He caught a turtle, or, some stories say, the turtle swam towards him, carrying in his mouth the golden sword of state. Le Loi at last accepted the signs, and used the sword to drive out the Chinese and found a new Vietnamese dynasty.

*   *   *

In the Philippines there was a similar tradition of fear of a powerful neighbour. The Philippine islands suffered particularly from Chinese pirates, and the retaliatory expeditions sent after the pirates by the south Chinese viceroys. The Spaniards did their best to segregate the small and harassed local Chinese communities; and later Filipino law was the exact opposite of Thai. A child took his father's nationality wherever he was born, and theoretically the grandchildren and great-grandchildren of Chinese immigrants who had married Filipino women stayed Chinese. But it was not a law that was generally observed in practice: and in recent years it has been noticed that, as in Thailand, many of the Filipinos who have talked most of the Chinese menace and pressed hardest for laws restricting the Chinese have been those who were themselves partly of Chinese descent.

* * *

Over the last few decades, however, the Chinese in most south-east Asian countries have been assimilated much more slowly than in the past. More sons and grandsons of immigrants have continued to speak Chinese, and think of themselves as Chinese, and many of these young men are the children of purely Chinese homes. In the twenties and the thirties of this century most families in China for the first time allowed wives to migrate with their husbands, or to join already established husbands or fiancés. Most of the south-east Asian governments welcomed the Chinese women and allowed them in on more generous quotas than were applied to Chinese men. The argument was that unmarried Chinese men led an unnatural life, Chinese labourers could not afford to marry local women, and, in Moslem countries, even if they had just enough money to support a wife, they found it difficult to get local girls to marry them. It was hoped that more Chinese family life would cut down on Chinese men's crimes of violence, opium smoking and gambling.

42

When they could find them, Chinese men, particularly first- and second-generation immigrants, preferred Chinese wives, especially if they came from their own village. In Thailand Chinese parents got 'milk money', the bride price, for a Chinese girl of three or four times that asked for an ordinary Thai peasant girl and sometimes twice that asked for a Lukjin, a half-Chinese and half-Thai woman. But in 1939 there was only one Chinese woman to every three men in Thailand and in Malaya; and even in Indonesia, the country with the biggest number of Chinese women, there was still a masculine majority. But these Chinese women did set a standard for the whole overseas community with homes as purely Chinese as they could be. A Chinese dialect was the first language their children learnt from their mothers; Chinese cooking, Chinese clothes and Chinese social customs were taken for granted.

The Chinese influence on the children of these homes was greatly increased if they went to one of the growing number of Chinese schools. Dr. William Skinner found in Thailand that the only fourth-generation Chinese who think of themselves as completely Chinese are those with a Chinese education. They have been taught in Chinese, by Chinese teachers, about Chinese subjects. Throughout south-east Asia the history and geography studied in Chinese schools are those of China, not those of the countries where the pupils actually live. The teachers, even when they avoid politics, are expected to teach patriotism for China. One well-known reading book for children starting school begins 'I am Chinese. I love my country. I live in Nanyang.' (Nanyang, or Southern Ocean, is the Chinese name for south-east Asia.)

In the early days of immigration there had been few Chinese schools, and those that existed were not particularly valued by businessmen fathers. They were schools in the traditional Chinese pattern where a major part of a child's education consisted of learning the Confucian classics by heart and chanting them back to his teacher. Successful self-made men often thought that a bright son could learn more and keep out of mischief better by starting work as soon as he was able.

But by the 1930s most Chinese parents had found that an education of some sort was increasingly valuable to their children in the new, more literate societies growing up in Asia; and Chinese schools in particular were much more popular than they had been. The classic Confucian texts had mostly been dropped in favour of more modern school books. Kuo-yu or 'Mandarin', the written version of the northern dialect, had replaced the far more complicated classical written language in south-east Asia as it had in China. As well as Chinese history and geography many schools offered business training, or at least taught their pupils the use of the Chinese abacus and general arithmetic.

Some of the popularity of these schools was because there was often no alternative education for Chinese children. Government-run primary schools, where they existed, taught children in the local language, not in Chinese, and anyway sometimes would not accept children of parents who were not recognised as nationals of the country. In Indonesia the Dutch opened government-run Chinese-Dutch schools with teaching in both languages. These schools were so popular that Chinese-Malay schools were also opened. Here intermediate classes allowed children to qualify for the Chinese-Dutch schools, and so, eventually, for university education in Holland.

6

1909: once Chinese always Chinese

WHAT was even more important to the speed of assimilation than the changes within the Chinese communities themselves, was the changing attitude in China towards emigrants. For several centuries the Chinese authorities forbade all emigration. Even the crews of trading junks who wanted to stay an extra year abroad had to have special permission. In 1712 the Ching court asked foreign governments to repatriate Chinese living abroad so that they could be executed for flouting their country's laws. There were in fact a few executions of returned emigrants during the 18th and 19th centuries, but mostly those who returned with enough money to bribe local officials were allowed to slip back into their villages. All the same, most scholarly opinion in China agreed with the government that emigrants were criminals or potential criminals, or at the best shockingly ungrateful for the favour of having been born Chinese. It was not an attitude that helped to bind successful emigrant Chinese to their home country.

By the beginning of the 20th century Chinese attitudes were changing. The intrusion of the western nations into China had shown that not all countries disowned their emigrants, and that the emigrants could exert valuable influence on behalf of their nations and send home useful amounts of foreign money. In 1909 the Ching court, in a last despairing attempt to avert revolution

45

by a front of modernity, passed a new nationality edict. It recognised children of Chinese fathers as Chinese wherever they were born, and it was to be the beginning of endless future trouble. To start with it was mostly ignored in south-east Asia. The Ching court was powerless to help or influence its nationals abroad, and the whole idea of nationality by blood contradicted the idea of territorial nationality (depending on where the child was born) current in several countries.

Meanwhile China's new revolutionaries, led by Dr. Sun Yat-sen, had been touring south-east Asian countries, raising money, giving promises of new attitudes in China, and generally rousing new interest and hope for effective home protection among the overseas communities. To some extent these new hopes were justified. The post-1911 governments did not forget the overseas Chinese. Ministers from the Kuomintang government at Nanking toured south-east Asia. The overseas Chinese were given special representatives in China, and an attempt was made to let them vote in Chinese national elections. Chinese diplomats interested themselves in the grievances and quarrels among the Chinese communities in the countries where they worked, and sometimes protested on their behalf to south-east Asian governments.

For their part the overseas Chinese strengthened their own ties with China. Money was raised for relief in China after national disasters, and China's war with Japan in the thirties was echoed in the boycotts of Japanese goods organised by the secret societies in the overseas Chinese communities. During the Second World War the Chinese, particularly in Malaya and Singapore, suffered forced labour and massacres at the hands of the Japanese because they were Chinese; and the most effective anti-Japanese resistance movements in Asia were largely Chinese-organised or dependent on help from the local Chinese communities.

46

However, China in the interwar and immediately post-war period was still too weak to be an effective protector of her nationals' interests. Her diplomatic protests to south-east Asian countries about the treatment of Chinese were ignored, visiting ministers snubbed and the boycott of Japanese goods declared illegal in several countries. The overseas Chinese might feel new sympathy for China, but it was hard to be proud of her and impossible to rely on her strength.

*　*　*

In 1948 Mao Tse-tung declared in Peking that 'the Chinese people have stood up'. It was a proud boast, more prosaically echoed for the overseas Chinese in an article in the *Ta Kung Pao* newspaper of Shanghai in January, 1950. 'Now that the People's Republic of China has been established ... the more than 10,000,000 overseas Chinese must not be subjected to further abuse.' China's rôle as the protector and the motherland of all Chinese was heavily stressed. The overseas Chinese were urged to return home and take part as all Chinese should in 'the glorious tasks of national reconstruction'. But those who preferred to remain overseas were not to be neglected. Peking Radio began to denounce any discrimination, anywhere in Asia, against the local Chinese. Overseas Chinese Commissions were set up in Peking and Canton, and overseas Chinese representatives of suitably left-wing political sympathies were elected to the People's Congresses at Peking.

What many overseas Chinese liked most about the new Communist China was the change in the popular foreign picture of the Chinese and their country. The past China had been a faintly comic country, always in trouble and governed inefficiently. The typical Chinese of western and much Asian imagination had been a fat, over-anxious and over-polite trader whose main peculiarity had been his inability to pronounce his 'r's'. The new China was often detested, but generally also feared and respected. The soldiers who fought in Korea and the young, hard officials of the new regime who worked sixteen hours a day were the newly typical Chinese citizens. All over Asia, even more than in the west, there was astonishment and envy at the communist government's successful campaigns for cleanliness and honesty, and China's growing industrialisation.

On the other hand overseas Chinese traders and businessmen, with firm ideas about the importance of private property and a man's duty to get on in the world, were the last people to sympathise with theoretical communism and the new Chinese idea that the most worthy people in society were those who had been the poorest workers and peasants. By 1950 the communist campaign against the landlords at its height, and Kangaroo trials, where the crowd howled for blood and the final sounds were the shots that ended the landlord's life, were broadcast over the Chinese radios. Overseas Chinese landholdings were safer than most; but many families in southeast Asia had relations killed in the purges, and others were shocked by the deaths or the taking away of all rights from landlords they had themselves known in China.

In Thailand Chiang Kai-shek's diplomats capitalised on the overseas Chinese horror at the mainland purges by organising remembrance services for relations and friends of local Chinese families who had been killed in China. But, even among the Chinese communities in Thailand, South Vietnam, the Philippines and Malaya, where the governments did not recognise the communists, Kuomintang newspapers were heavily subsidised, and where, at times, Chiang's diplomats were allowed to work with the police on anti-communist purges of the local Chinese communities, the Kuomintang was never a particularly popular alternative to communists. Overseas Chinese remembered the anarchy of post-war China, and rumours out of Taiwan did not suggest that the Kuomintang was learning much in exile.

During the period of the purges there was a heavy drop in overseas Chinese remittances to their families. This was less a reaction to general policies than to news coming from China of the blackmailing methods used by local officials on the families who had had remittances. They were threatened (and sometimes the threats were carried out) with imprisonment, torture or killing if they did not write to their rich relations in foreign countries and ask for more money. Letters were drafted for them to sign, and the money that came back was not only useful foreign exchange for the government, but the families in China were urged, under threat of further punishment, to use it to buy state bonds or contribute towards officially sponsored charities. Exit permits for wives and old parents were made dependent, in many cases, on overseas Chinese sending home impossibly large sums of money. Other Chinese from abroad, returning to China on short visits, were questioned about how much they earned, and sometimes told to ask for higher wages so as to be able to send more to their home villages. When the overseas Chinese found that bigger remittances only increased this sort of blackmail and endangered their families, many of them stopped sending money altogether.

By 1952 the Chinese government had realised its mistake. Local officials were ordered not to interfere with remittances, blackmail of families stopped and an increasing amount of money was in consequence sent from overseas back to China. Sometimes this money was sent, through Hong Kong, against the laws of the countries where the overseas Chinese were living. Neither the south-east Asian countries nor the United States with its

Chinese community on the west coast were ever able to stop overseas Chinese supporting their families in China when they wanted to do so.

Meanwhile as the worst of the purges finished in China, and there was more news of communist material achievements, the overseas Chinese began to hear more about the privileges China was prepared to offer returning members of their communities. Temporary visitors from overseas, particularly those organised in official parties and invited delgations, could arrange to be met by Intourist guides at the Hong Kong frontier. Shumchun, where they waited for the train to Canton, is one of the cleanest railway stations in Asia. The bookstalls there are piled with free magazines illustrating the work of the new government. Loudspeaker music is piped all over the station, interspersed with Peking news and slogans and exhortations to the crowd to behave in a clean and orderly way. For important visitors customs formalities are mostly waived. Their waiting room is furnished with white antimacassars, imitation leather armchairs, a lace tablecloth and heavily polished brass spittoons—all in the Victorian manner so much admired in many overseas Chinese homes. When the Canton train arrived, visitors noted, or their Intourist guides pointed out to them, that the train was on time, spotlessly clean, and with an attendant in a white face-mask whose one job it was to mop up any litter that might be dropped during the journey. The Shumchun station staff stood to attention as the train pulled out, and the loudspeakers played martial music.

All visitors were taken round the southern showplaces of the new regime: the new factories round Canton, the state store (packed with the industrial and consumer goods the new industries were beginning to turn out), a new housing estate and a model village where the leaders of the peasants' co-operatives assured the visitors that agricultural output had risen and the people were better off than ever before.

If overseas Chinese visitors had time they were always encouraged to visit the new factories opening in Manchuria, and to go to Peking where the communists had restored most of the famous monuments. For many overseas visitors the effect of what they saw was heightened by the untrue or exaggerated stories that the Kuomintang and some American propagandists were circulating about China. Political oppression was kept out of sight, and there was obviously neither mass famine nor chaos in the country they were visiting.

Some members of the overseas Chinese community were more than temporary visitors to the new China. Over the last fifty years it had become an overseas Chinese tradition in many groups that those emigrants who could afford it sent their children home for a Chinese education in China. Life in Communist China was made as easy as possible for these students. Scholarships were sometimes offered to them, there were special schools where students could be coached up to university standards, university places were reserved for them, and schools and colleges with overseas students were given extra food rations and new buildings.

Like all Chinese university students, whatever else they were studying the young men and women from overseas took communist theory and the Russian language as compulsory courses; and they attended a certain number of political meetings and 'study groups' on the part they should themselves play in the work of the new government. Their ambition normally was to be allowed to join the Communist Party. Overseas students were expected to write letters home to their friends and families about the advantages of their lives in China, and how much communism had helped everybody. Many of them planned to return to south-east Asia at the end of their courses, but the south-east Asian governments were increasingly reluctant to allow them back. However, even students who could not return to their homes were useful to the Chinese government because they knew south-east Asian languages and conditions in the countries there.

Older overseas Chinese with some money, who wanted to retire to south China, were welcomed by the new government because of the foreign exchange they brought home, and their propaganda value. A special village was set up for them as a suburb of Canton. The families there designed their own houses, they were offered good general welfare facilities, and there was a school for their children. The Chinese radios and newspapers, while circulating news of this village, also stressed that poorer men and the relations of overseas Chinese families were given privileged positions in the new village co-operatives. They were not pressed to work as long a day as other peasants, and if they were former landlords, they were allowed to change their 'class status' faster than usual and regain their civil rights.

Overseas Chinese were also encouraged to invest in the new China. They were offered 8 per cent interest on their money, which was to be spent on building new factories round Canton, and on other state-sponsored projects. There were promises that whatever happened to other private investment in China, overseas Chinese investments would continue to pay interest at the promised rate. After Chinese investors had hesitated for some months the company was attracting enough money to finance several Canton factories from the overseas communities.

7

Post-war tension in south-east Asia

WHILE China was strengthening her ties with the overseas Chinese communities, other Asian countries were growing increasingly frightened of her and of communism generally. The new effectiveness of Chinese power was shown by the Chinese armies in Korea against U.N. forces that included a detachment from Thailand. After the Korean War there were recurrent crises, hovering on the edge of open fighting, over the American protection of Formosa; the war in Indochina intensified, and the Vietminh invaded Laos; and in 1954 Thailand and the Philippines—countries which already received substantial American aid—joined SEATO. Peking Radio threatened that the 'American satellites' would suffer as all China's enemies were bound to suffer. The new China, said the radio commentators, was a great and powerful nation, and the SEATO countries had brought war and their own annihilation nearer.

To add to the tension the south-east Asian governments had their own internal difficulties. These they generally blamed on the immediately post-war decision of the Communist Party to try for power all over south-east Asia; and, often less fairly, on Chinese intervention on behalf of local communists in their countries. Overseas Chinese were seen increasingly as natural communists, and as Peking's fifth column in an attempt to extend China's borders south to Indonesia and west to India.

(This was the area that some communist-published maps labelled 'China'.)

*   *   *

In Malaya there was only a short interval of peace after the end of the world war before the local 'terrorists' began their civil war by killing Chinese and European civilians and destroying rubber plantations. Most of the 'terrorists' to begin with were ex-wartime guerrillas, who had kept their weapons, and used their old jungle hide-outs for the new war. There was never any evidence of Peking's giving direct orders to these men, or supplying them with arms, and no Chinese advisers were ever found.

Like other of the post-war communist rebel groups in Asia, the Malayan terrorists were more influenced by the Soviet Union than by China. Their political leaders emphasised the rôle of the Russians as 'elder brothers' and examples for communists everywhere. In the in-doctrination courses and study groups held in the jungle the required reading was from Lenin's and Stalin's works rather than Mao Tse-tung's, and students were encour-aged to draw comparisons from Russian rather than Chinese history. But in the 1950s the success of com-munism in China certainly encouraged the Malayan communists to hope that communism might be equally successful in their country, and there was an increasing use of propaganda examples taken from China and the catch-phrases popularised by Peking.

The use of Peking catch-phrases and some of the propaganda methods used in China was even more marked among the communist-inclined older school-children in Singapore. Communist cells were organised in the schools, and study groups held under the guidance of the older students—some of whom were in their twenties and believed to be trained in methods of politi-cal agitation. In the mid-1950s there were strikes in the

Chinese secondary schools when students barricaded themselves in the classrooms and the police had to use tear gas to evict them. Students also led processions outside the schools, some of which culminated in riots where young people and the police were killed and injured. The ostensible cause of these riots and strikes were local grievances, like the attempt to call up Singapore young men for a very limited form of national service; but there was also a general background of extreme anti-colonialism, a desire to make things difficult for the politically moderate leaders of Singapore of all races, and a sympathy for the Malayan terrorists and their aims.

Communism in the schools was encouraged by the number of textbooks students used which were printed either in China or by communist presses in Hong Kong. Chinese dictionaries carried the obvious communist examples for the use of words: for 'band together' in a Peking-printed text the example given is—'in the past the tyrannous landlords and the reactionary government banded together to bully and oppress the people'. But the more ingenious examples of careful communist writing are saved for the apparently less political subjects. In a junior arithmetic textbook children learning addition are shown how to add up the aid given by Russia to China. In the Chinese classics, introductions and drastic editing are used to ram home political lessons. The Peking edition of *The Records of the Travels of an Old Cripple*, one of the most popular Chinese novels, has an explanatory note: 'Liu Neo (the author) was opposed to the revolutionary forces of his time. Hence his book contains portions which condemn or attack the revolutionaries. That is a defect. During the process of checking and revising we have trimmed down or deleted the reactionary chapters, paragraphs and phrases to about one-tenth of the original book.'

The Singapore government, when they collected examples like these from the colony's schoolbooks, noted that the wholesale banning of books from communist houses was not possible, because there were no alternative texts students could use in their normal studies and examinations.

When the school riots and the Malayan Terrorist movement were at their height, many Malays and some British officials were reluctant to believe that Peking was not more directly connected with the details of local communism than she was. This was partly because it was easier to blame Malaya and Singapore's troubles on the machinations of China rather than on local grievances and perhaps local inefficiency. Moreover the unpopularity of China and all Chinese was added to by the genuine involvement of many of the local Malayan Chinese in the terrorism and the school riots. The terrorists killed more Chinese than members of any other community, but nearly all the terrorists and all the rioting students were Chinese, and the terrorists could not have continued their jungle warfare without the supplies and information given them, willingly or unwillingly, by the ordinary Chinese population.

The need to protect those Chinese who helped the terrorists because they were threatened was the official reason given for moving large numbers of small Chinese farmers from the scattered farms where they had been squatting without legal claim to their land. During the early 1950s these farmers were grouped in walled villages with armed guards who followed them into fields to stop anything being passed from a villager to a terrorist. Unfortunately a few officials and some Chinese saw these villages as a form of punishment for past Chinese collaboration with the terrorists. There was stress sometimes on restrictions which stopped any food being taken into the fields—even a bowl of rice for the farmer to eat at midday. There were complaints about the new land the farmers had been given; and, in spite of the walls and the police in some villages the guard was so bad that farmers were killed after they had refused to give rice to terrorists who climbed in on supply expeditions.

Among the educated Chinese there was considerable resentment at the Malayan and Singapore emergency regulations. Chinese were arrested whom the local community believed were not communists, but merely aggrieved students or men with liberal or socialist opinions. Intercommunal tension increased with Malay resentment of the difficulties the Chinese were bringing to the country, and there were slogans among reputable political parties of 'Malaya for the Malays' and 'foreigners— go home'. There was Malay opposition to attempts to recruit more Chinese for the local civil service and the police, and to attempts to make it easier for Chinese to become Malayan citizens.

New Chinese immigration into Malaya practically stopped after the 1953 Act which laid down that the only aliens who would be allowed into the country were professional men or women and artisans who were assured of work in Malaya. The Malayan Chinese Association, commenting on the new Act, said that it was 'apparently being used as a political weapon to restrict the number of Chinese living in Malaya'. In Singapore only the wives and families of Chinese already in the colony or 'those who can contribute to the commerce and industry of the colony or who can provide specialised services' were to be admitted. As in Malaya this clause was interpreted so as to allow in only an occasional handful of Chinese immigrants.

*　　*　　*

The French in Indochina produced more suggestive evidence of Peking aid to the Vietminh communist armies than the British were ever able to produce for the Malayan terrorists. In 1950 when the Chinese communist armies reached south-west China, and for the first time shared a frontier with the Vietminh forces of North Vietnam, the Vietminh also mounted their first major offensive against the French armies, turning from harassing guerrilla action to the seizure of cities and open battles. Peking radio commentators talked with more enthusiasm, less caution, and far more often about the Vietnamese war than they did about the Malayan; China was the first country to recognise the Vietminh as a legal government; and at one period the French prime minister, René Pleven, claimed that 20,000 Vietminh troops had been trained and equipped in China. Other Frenchmen pointed out the convenience to China of the Vietminh offensives which tied up western troops and equipment during the Korean War.

Nevertheless the presence of Chinese officers with the Vietminh was never conclusively proved, and the Vietminh claimed that the Chinese artillery and small-arms they had were legally bought from China—generally through Hong Kong. There were in any case limits to the type of arms China was prepared to supply to the Vietminh. There was no Vietminh air force for instance, although with bombing planes the Vietminh victory over the French could probably have been much quicker and more decisive.

During the Vietnamese war the local Chinese community managed to remain fairly neutral. They were proud of the new respect all Vietnamese had to have for China, but they disliked the war conditions that made trade difficult. When the Geneva agreement was eventually concluded, most of the northern Chinese traders preferred to be evacuated to the south, with its freer conditions for traders, rather than stay on in the new communist region. All the same the southern government did not trust them. Old Vietnamese fears of Chinese domination were given new substance by what most South Vietnamese saw as the virtual Chinese overlordship over the communist north of their country. Vietnamese said that China would be ready to go to greater lengths to foster communism in Vietnam than in most other parts of south-east Asia, because she would be glad to have a satellite state on her south-western frontier. The increasingly powerful leaders of South Vietnam pressed the French to withdraw their privileges from the local Chinese community; and there was an increased control of Chinese schools, movement and settlement.

* * *

In the post-war Philippines, another newly independent country, Chinese who had fled from the Japanese occupation of the islands were refused automatic re-admission to the country. Many of them tried to bribe their way on to the tiny Chinese immigration quota. While the Chinese then blamed the Filipinos for excluding them, as they thought, unjustly, the Filipinos blamed the Chinese for trying to bypass the country's laws.

The Huks, the communist-inspired rebels of the Philippines, were Filipinos; although there was some evidence of the local Chinese community giving them help. But most of the political restrictions on the Chinese and the deportations of the Chinese were concerned less with the Huks than the government's fear of Peking-inspired plots, and desire to stand well with the Americans and so with the American-allied government of Chiang Kai-shek.

Economically it was becoming increasingly difficult for a Chinese to carry on a business in the Philippines. The middle rank of Chinese particularly disliked the regulation of 1954 that when the alien owner of a shop died his business must be sold up. This meant that not only could the son of a Chinese shopkeeper not inherit his father's business; but also that when a Chinese shopkeeper died suddenly his family were likely to lose heavily in their forced, quick sale.

* * *

Post-war Thailand was not troubled by large-scale internal rebellions. But in 1947 Pridi Phanomyong, whose liberal government had been markedly sympathetic to the local Chinese, was replaced, first by a government of conservative civilians, and then by Marshal Phibun heading a military and police clique. Before the war Phibun had been responsible for a number of restrictions on Thai Chinese; and he was a firm ally of the United States, and a pledged anti-communist. His fear of China and communism was increased when the Chinese communists started a 'Thai autonomous area' in the provinces that bordered Thailand, and when Pridi, after a mysterious disappearance, reappeared in Peking and talked to Thais over Peking radio. In 1953 and 1954 there were strong rumours about the spread of a communist-inspired 'Free Thai' movement in north Thailand.

Marshal Phibun, like the other south-east Asian leaders, saw particular dangers in the economic power of the Thai Chinese. Patriotic Thais were urged to 'Thai-ify' the country's economy by eating only food that was produced by Thais, wearing clothing manufactured by Thais, and assisting other Thais to enter trade and industry. Thais were urged to enter the new government-run vocational schools so as to be able to compete with 'aliens'. More and more trades and occupations were closed to Chinese, sometimes at a few days' notice. Chinese rice milling, tobacco trading and meat marketing were all restricted. The Chinese were forbidden to buy land, and certain areas of Thailand were closed to all Chinese residents.

There had been pre-war Thai restrictions on Chinese schools, but in the immediate post-war period new schools had opened. The governors now shut down the majority of these under threat of fines, arrests and deportations for a breach of Phibun's new regulations. Those schools that remained open were not allowed to devote enough time to Chinese to see that their pupils spoke, let alone wrote and read, the language properly.

In a Thai purge, aimed avowedly at communists, in 1952 several hundred Chinese were arrested who later had to be released because there was no evidence against them. The alien registration fee was increased twenty times to a sum that was almost impossible for the poorer Chinese to pay. There was an officially sponsored anti-Chinese campaign in the newspapers; and, what was potentially most important of all, Thailand's traditionally tolerant nationality policy was reversed. It was no longer possible for second-generation Chinese born in Thailand to become Thai citizens automatically. Instead a number of conditions had to be satisfied, and local officials were particularly warned to investigate carefully cases of non-Thais who tried to slip into citizenship by taking Thai names.

* * *

In Burma, partly because the Chinese community was so small, trouble with China and local communist rebellions did not lead to reprisals against the overseas Chinese community. But there was a growing fear of China's intentions, and pressure on the Burmese government to stop illegal Chinese immigration into Burma. The biggest Sino-Burmese crisis was over the defeated units of the Kuomintang armies which had crossed into Burma and established themselves in the troubled hill regions. The soldiers used their hill retreats as bases to raid back into China and into the Burma plains. Peking threatened to send her own armies over the border to clean out the Kuomintang units if the Burmese army could not do this themselves. Meanwhile maps, drawn up in Peking, were circulating showing large areas of Burmese hill territory as within the Chinese frontier. On the Burmese plains the Rangoon government had both orthodox communist rebellions to deal with, and local bandits who claimed to be communists or Trotskyists, apparently in the hope of adding a certain respectability to their robberies.

*　　*　　*

Indonesia might in theory have been the most tolerant of all south-east Asian countries to its Chinese community. Unlike the Chinese of Malaya and Thailand, the Indonesian Chinese were a small minority in the total population. There was no open communist trouble in Indonesia, but instead the first rebellions in independent Indonesia were from the right wing—inspired by religious fanaticism or movements of local separatists.

Indonesia is not a member of SEATO. She was one of the first countries to recognise Peking and, on the whole, Indonesians are particularly sympathetic to China's dislike of the western colonial nations, and her attempts to become a great power and industrialise herself. But the Indonesians never felt themselves able to trust their local Chinese, or forgive the way that many Chinese merchants had sided with the Dutch during the post-war nationalist struggles. The Chinese community on their side found it hard to forget the wanton killing of Chinese families and destruction of Chinese property by Indonesian nationalists during the civil war. In June 1946 6,000 Chinese in the Tangerang area had been murdered and had their homes burned because of Indonesian suspicions that they were collaborating with the Dutch, and there had been similar incidents, although on a smaller scale, over the next four years.

In 1953 the Indonesian government announced that in future the Dutch 'open door' policy on Chinese immigration would be reversed, and strict quotas applied to the Chinese. For Chinese businessmen already in Indonesia, life became increasingly difficult. Shop signs written in Chinese were forbidden, and confused shopkeepers kept within the letter of the law when they had their signs re-written, not in Indonesian, but in English. Chinese firms could not get import or export licences. Even the queues of Chinese in government offices, waiting for the many forms needed by any businessman in Indonesia, moved more slowly and were treated more rudely by officials than the Indonesian native queues.

8

Change in Chinese policy

In the mid-1950s south-east Asia had very little to offer overseas Chinese who were wavering in their loyalties. Most of the countries were plagued by rebellions; and it was often unsafe to travel in the remoter districts because of the dangers of rebel ambushes on the roads and railways, as well as the more normal dangers of being killed or robbed by ordinary criminals.

Even the most ordinary government services did not work. Somewhat later in the decade U Nu, the Burman prime minister, complained to a planning seminar that the Rangoon telephone system would respond neither to 'prayer nor abuse'. Far too many officials had to be bribed before they would do their work; and in the most strongly anti-communist countries the police had a financially useful threat to hold over the heads of the local Chinese. Unless money was given to the police the Chinese would be accused of communism, and would then face inevitable inconvenience, prison, deportation or perhaps death.

Unpredictable and bad government and ill-feeling against the Chinese survived the fifties. But most Asians, including the overseas Chinese, date an improvement in their post-war history from the 1955 Afro-Asian conference at Bandung. At the conference Chou En-lai represented China in a new and more moderate rôle: and among the causes of international tension he was prepared to discuss was the position of the overseas Chinese communities in south-east Asia. The most important result of these discussions was the dual-nationality treaty he negotiated with Indonesia. It offered the Indonesian Chinese a choice between Chinese nationality or Indonesian nationality recognised by China. It was the first time a Chinese government had officially allowed that the son of a Chinese father could stop being a Chinese citizen.

It was a complicated treaty, and it was to be five years before it was ratified; but at the time of Bandung it was one of the most widely quoted bits of evidence of the generally more peaceful atmosphere, and China's more liberal policies both at home and abroad. The Chinese stress at Bandung and for some years afterwards was on the United Front of all Asian nations, the need for everybody to accept criticism from everybody, and on 'The Five Principles' for peaceful co-existence agreed on by Chou En-lai and Nehru. But by 1958, although some of the same forms of words were still being used, Chinese policies at home and abroad had hardened.

Abroad after 1957–58 there was new stress on the wiles of American imperialism, the inevitable correctness of Chinese policy, and the continuing conflict that must of necessity exist between eastern socialism and western capitalism. China re-painted the west in old-fashioned Stalinist terms as ever-decadent, colonialist and war-mongering. The Chinese people were told that a threat by the west anywhere in the world was a threat against China. Whatever interests China's arch enemy, the United States, had in the world were interests against China. A war of capitalism and communism was probably inevitable, but China because of her vast hinterland was the country that would lose least by such a war. It was generally believed to be Chinese pressure on Khruschev for a 'hard' policy and no concessions to the west, and their support for diehard Stalinists in Russia, that led to the wreck of the Summit Conference and the partial renewal of the cold war in 1960.

In Asia the most dramatic instances of the harder Chinese policy were the suppression of the Tibetan rebellion and the Chinese incursions over the Indian frontier. Most Asians were horrified by the news from Tibet and the flight of the Dalai Lama. Tibet was an Asian country whose independence had been generally recognised outside China for over a hundred years: a longer history of independence than most south-east Asian countries possessed. The Tibetan invasion was labelled Chinese imperialism even by formerly neutralist newspapers in Burma and Indonesia and a great deal of space was given to what details of it were available. In contrast outside India there was less interest in the question of whether India or China were in the right over the boundaries of their Himalayan frontier.

Possibly south-east Asians were wrong in the relative importance they attached to these two Chinese actions. In Tibet China considered that she was only taking her own again. Strong Chinese emperors always had controlled Tibet and tried to use the Dalai and the Panchen Lamas as their puppets. Over the Indian frontier China again believed she was in the right, and had maps and documents to support her claim to some of the Himalayan regions generally included in India. On the other hand her manner of putting forward her claims and the capture and torture of Indian troops was as provocative as it could be, and may have been caused by a new willingness to pick a quarrel with India: perhaps because of Chinese fury at the asylum India had given to the Dalai Lama, perhaps because of the growing Chinese realisation that India was her main rival in Asia—the more dangerous because her international mildness and her neutrality made her particularly attractive to other Asian neutral nations.

However, the quarrel with India did not affect south-east Asia directly, and on the whole the Chinese con-

66

tinued to behave in a conciliatory manner towards most south-east Asian nations. This was partly because in the post-Bandung world the Chinese seem to have lost interest in south-east Asia. Chinese diplomats apparently decided that the imperialists' main interests, and therefore the Chinese conflict with them, now centred on Africa and South America. Smaller Asian delegations and larger Arab and Latin American delegations were invited to the May Day celebrations in China. Peking radio devoted less time to denouncing counter-revolution and imperialism in south-east Asia and more to 'the revolutionary struggles' in Guatemala, Cuba, the Congo or Algeria. Chinese diplomats able to speak classical Arabic were sent to talk to President Nasser, and diplomats who could quote from the most acceptable Spanish classics went to Latin America. South-east Asia was left with second-rank men who were instructed to emphasise the continuing Asian United Front, and the peaceful intentions of China.

In this policy of the Asian United Front the overseas Chinese were on the whole an embarrassment. For the time being the best service they could render was to keep out of trouble, and become, at least on the surface, good citizens of south-east Asian countries. In 1957 Chou En-lai advised the Chinese of Burma to become Burmese citizens on the very easy terms offered by the Burmese government. Chinese schools, he said, should teach Burmese, and adult Chinese should make every effort to learn their new language. Those former Chinese who became Burmans should not take part in activities organised by the overseas Chinese. Those who kept their Chinese nationality should not interfere in Burmese politics. Chinese in Burma should invest in local industries; and China, Chou promised, would not recruit communists from among the overseas Chinese.

In February 1958 Madame Ho Hsiang-ning laid down

a more general version of how the overseas Chinese should behave. In her speech to the National People's Congress in Peking Madame Ho said: 'we hold that overseas Chinese should be free to choose the nationality of the country in which they reside and should be loyal to that country and its people. As for those who wish to remain Chinese subjects, we ask them to continue to observe the policies, laws and regulations of their countries of residence and to respect the customs and habits of the local people. Overseas Chinese should be encouraged to invest commercial capital in local industries, and to co-operate with native capitalists to help develop the independent national economies of the countries in which they live. Children of overseas Chinese should study local languages, geography and history, and acquire certain skills so that they may enter higher schools or earn a living there.'

*   *   *

Meanwhile at home in China during this period, 'the hundred flowers' of liberal criticism were officially said to be in need of weeding and pruning. The more violent of the government's critics were silenced, and there was new stress on the need for intellectuals to conform to the communist ideal, and strengthen their ties with the proletariat. Everywhere there were longer hours devoted to political study; and, particularly in universities, schools and offices, meetings devoted to self-criticism about the failure, as the communist leaders called it, of many intellectuals during the hundred flowers period. Students and schoolchildren were now expected to spend several weeks of their holidays on farms or in factories, fraternising with, and putting in at least as hard a day as, the regular peasants and workers.

In this newer, stricter China of the late 1950s overseas Chinese residents or visitors were as much of an embarrassment on the home scene as their communities were abroad. There was less and less room for students bred in western opinions, or for old people who wanted to retire after a lifetime of very un-communist petty trading, saving and making small profits. There was new emphasis in the official statements on the need for 'the long ideological education' of those who had lived abroad; and overseas Chinese were no longer excepted, as they had been in the old days, from the longest sessions of political study and the most searching bouts of self-criticism.

Students from overseas had fewer special school and college places reserved for them than in the past. The universities they went to no longer had better food than the average, and priorities for new buildings and they were not excepted from the obligation to do manual work. Several groups of students returned from China to their homes in south-east Asia with discontented stories of sleeping in overcrowded dormitories, eating badly and not being able to work in their chosen fields of study.

Overseas students, it was apparently argued in Peking, no longer had the same value for China while she followed her United Front policy with south-east Asia. They were not wanted as potential communist organisers in their own countries; or, while the main energies of Chinese foreign policy were directed elsewhere, as new members of south-east Asian departments in Peking publishing houses or in the Chinese foreign office.

Meanwhile the financial value to China of all the overseas communities was lessening as the remittances from abroad dropped. This was partly because the main stream of immigration had stopped about 1950, and it had always been the newest arrivals in south-east Asia who had naturally been most concerned about the families they had recently left. But the drying-up of remittances also reflected the horror felt by many of the older generation of Chinese at some of the changes under communism in China: particularly the changes in country life.

The commune movement had spread to south China, and money sent by the overseas Chinese to their families could no longer be used to help small family farms or even village co-operatives. These had been swallowed into the enormous, countrywide communes with thousands of member-families and no private ownership of land. Traditional family life was threatened as the commune officials urged women out to work in the fields or the new factories. Young children, the most enthusiastic officials said, should be left in the commune's nurseries, and the old cared for in special 'Happiness Homes' instead of waited on in their family houses by dutiful daughters-in-law. Food was cooked in communal mess halls, and in some of the most 'advanced' communes sewing brigades relieved the wife even from the duty of mending the family's clothes.

* * *

Not all overseas Chinese are however even now equally disillusioned about the new government of their country. It is still true that many of the young overseas Chinese particularly are often very proud of their nationality, and prefer to identify themselves with the puritan severity of a world power, rather than the small-scale and sometimes ineffective governments of the countries they were born in. Nor has China herself abandoned all interest in the overseas communities. This is at least partly due to the continued existence of Formosa and the recognition of Chiang Kai-shek's Kuomintang government there not only by the United States but also by the American allied south-east Asian countries—South Vietnam, Laos, Thailand and the Philippines. Even if China decided to abandon any future hopes she may have of using the overseas Chinese as a fifth column in Asia she still cannot afford to ignore their interests and so let it be said that the Kuomintang rump cares more for general Chinese interests than does the Communist Party. If Peking ignored the interests of even the most bourgeois, small shopkeeper section of the overseas Chinese communities, the Kuomintang might gain new adherents from their relatives in south China, or might profit from more investment and remittances from the overseas communities themselves, and Peking would lose international and national prestige. This has meant that paradoxically Peking has lent weight to Formosa's position in southeast Asia.

As an effective protector on her own of overseas Chinese interests Formosa would be negligible. Internationally Formosa has only a nuisance value, and her protests would carry no weight if they were not inevitably partnered or followed by equally vehement and much more weighty protests from Peking.

A second result has been that while Formosa continues to offer facilities for investment, tours, retirement and study under the influence of the Kuomintang, Peking has to offer at least equal facilities—however inconvenient the overseas Chinese may be in the new China. Official Peking announcements still say that a Chinese returning to China will be welcomed like 'an orphan coming back to the arms of its mother'. In 1959, although the stress on orthodoxy was greater than ever in China, the Vice-Chairman of the Kwantung Provincial Overseas Chinese Affairs Committee carefully listed all that China was still offering to her overseas citizens. And, however hedged with restrictions these Chinese facilities are, all over south-east Asia there are still more young men and women who want to study in China rather than in Formosa, and more of their elders feel that their loyalties, their investment and their real homes are in China however much they disapprove of some of the government actions there.

The same need to prevent Formosa, and the Kuomintang's American backers, from securing the loyalties of the overseas Chinese community means that Peking propaganda has often contradicted her official advice that the overseas Chinese should become good citizens of the countries they are domiciled in. Communist-influenced textbooks continue to be distributed cheaply to south-east Asian Chinese schools. In an album found in a Chinese girls' school in Sarawak in 1959 one of the songs ran:

> *The People's suffering is as deep as the sea.*
> *They long for liberation day and night.*
> *The Chinese Communist Party is like the red sun;*
> *By its strength it liberates others.*
> *Welcome to the comfort mission of our Fatherland.*

There is an even more closely fought competition between Formosa and the Chinese communists over Chinese newspapers in south-east Asia and Chinese listeners to radio programmes. On the whole it is a competition which the Chinese communists have won by greater technical skill, and because they can print and broadcast news from the south Chinese villages from which the overseas Chinese come. For Asian newspapers aiming at neutrality the communist-sponsored China News Service is less blatantly filled with propaganda than the equivalent Formosan news service; Peking's China News Service is also cheaper than most western services, and is specially edited with an eye to the particular interests and prejudices of the overseas Chinese communities.

Several of the south-east Asian countries do their best to prevent newspapers directly subsidised by Formosa or Peking being published in their territory. The difficulty has always been to find out which newspapers are receiving subsidies—so many Chinese newspapers in south-east Asia seem to have uneconomically small circulations. In Rangoon in 1959 there were four pro-communist newspapers all with circulations of less than five thousand, and one pro-Kuomintang newspaper, with a smaller circulation still, and notably worse printed and worse staffed than its rivals.

* * *

China's trade offensive in the late 1950s was motivated, less by rivalry with Formosa, than by rivalry with Japan, and the Chinese need for foreign exchange. Japan was a wartime enemy turned American ally, her government had refused to recognise Peking, and her industrial successes were often quoted by neutral and western sources to belittle the progress made in China. By 1958 Japanese newspapers estimated that new Chinese consumer goods, like cotton cloth, paper, china and glass, were sold 30 to 40 per cent more cheaply than similar goods produced in Japan. Except in countries like South Vietnam where trade with China was illegal, Chinese goods were steadily taking south-east Asian markets away from Japanese goods. In Hong Kong shirts made in China sold for around 5s., an electric torch for 2s. 6d. and children's shoes for 7s. 9d.

Western goods also suffered in the competition with China. In Kuala Lumpur in 1958 a British-made bicycle cost £12 10s. against £5 for a Chinese bicycle. The same £5 Kuala Lumpur bicycle however sold for £25 in Shanghai, and it was generally believed that China was securing her markets by selling below cost price.

China could not however keep up the 1958 flow of goods into south-west Asia, and by 1959 some Hong Kong shippers were claiming that Chinese goods had not arrived on the promised dates and were not always of

73

the promised quality. But each month new Chinese factories started to turn out new items—surgical instruments, new machinery, industrial goods. Even small quantities of goods like these added greatly to Chinese prestige in south-east Asia where every nation had plans to industrialise, and the products of heavy industry have all the glamour associated only with handicrafts in the over-factoried west.

Overseas Chinese merchants are mostly proud of this new national prestige, and they also want a sure supply of the cheap goods produced in China. The goods are sold when possible through the commercial sections of the local Chinese embassies, and the control this gives the embassies over merchants is added to by the loans, arranged on very easy terms by the branches of the Peking-run Bank of China. Few Chinese merchants can get loans on such low interest rates and such easy terms from rival western banks, but the Bank of China makes an ample political, if not an economic, profit out of its money. Loans do not go to notorious supporters of the Kuomintang; and it is believed, in Burma particularly, that some of the conditions of the Bank of China's loans are that the merchants' children shall go to the most communist-orientated of the local Chinese schools, and his family subscribe to the most orthodox of the local communist newspapers.

9

The south-east Asian governments after Bandung

IN the post-Bandung period several Asian governments responded to the easier Chinese policies and their own greater internal security by modifying their policies about their overseas Chinese communities. The most marked change was in Thailand whose foreign minister had been assured by Chou En-lai at Bandung that the Chinese Thai Autonomous Area was not meant as a threat to Thailand.

It was also obvious that Marshal Phibun's plan to replace Chinese shopkeepers and traders by Thais had failed, and government departments and the police were increasingly turning a blind eye to the use of Thai 'front men' who allowed their names to be used to shelter the Chinese who really continued to control the businesses from which they were legally barred. These Thai directors in the old purely Chinese firms were chosen mostly because of their influence with the police and the government and the protection they were ready to sell their Chinese colleagues.

During 1956 Thai newspapers suddenly dropped their previous abuse of the Chinese community to stress the contribution the Chinese had made to Thailand, and the registration fee for aliens was reduced. The new tough Nationality Act was modified both legally and in administrative practice. Chinese with Thai wives or who had had Thai mothers were almost begged by local officials to take Thai nationality; and in 1956 a new electoral law gave Thai citizens with alien fathers the right, for the first time, to stand for election to the National Assembly.

There is however a continued repression of the Chinese schools in Thailand. Very little time is allowed for Chinese language teaching in these schools, and the Thai government rigidly controls what textbooks can be used and what teachers employed in them. The result has been that for its numbers the Thai Chinese community has fewer and smaller Chinese schools than the Chinese communities of other south-east Asian countries.

* * *

Because Malaya was still a colony at the time of Bandung there were no Malayan representatives at the Conference. But the leaders of the new nation when Malaya became independent in 1957 were influenced both by the Peking policy of encouraging the assimilation of overseas Chinese communities, and by the virtual ending of their own 'emergency', leaving only a handful of communist guerrillas still fighting from remote jungle hideouts. In the country's new constitution any discrimination on the grounds of race or religion was declared illegal, although special privileges of employment in some sorts of jobs and in land ownership were still reserved for Malays. There was Malay pressure, too, against what was considered over-easy citizenship for the Chinese. But the new constitution still offered fairly generous terms. Chinese already in the country were allowed to become Malayan citizens after eight years of residence, and children born in the Malayan Federation after its independence were automatically Malayan citizens whatever their parents' race.

The new government of the Federation was a coalition

of Chinese, Indian and Malay parties under the able and tolerant Malay Prime Minister, Tungku Abdul Rahman. The Chinese Party, the Malayan Chinese Association, had even more influence than the number of Chinese voters in the Federation indicated. The leaders of other parties were afraid that unless concessions were made to Chinese opinion, the leadership of the Chinese might pass from the M.C.A. moderates to the more violently partisan or left-wing Chinese parties.

In the Chinese squatters' villages conditions were also easier as the emergency ended and the more rigid restrictions were relaxed. The Malayan loyalties of many of the Chinese farmers were strengthened as they realised that the new villages gave them their first secure land-holdings. New schools, clinics and village halls were set up, so that the Chinese were often better provided with amenities than surrounding Malay villagers. Agricultural officers had encouraged new crops and new methods in the squatter villages and as they tested them many of the farmers found them profitable and time-saving.

* * *

Of all the south-east Asian countries South Vietnam was the most dependent on its status as an anti-communist country, and the American aid it received. To the old feuds with the Chinese and new suspicions that the local Chinese community might be fifth columnists for either China herself or for Communist North Vietnam were added nationalist feelings inflamed by Peking and Hanoi accusations that the country was 'an American satellite'.

In 1956 and 1957 the South Vietnamese government attempted to close a number of occupations to the Chinese, including the rice trade which had been almost entirely Chinese-run. The local Chinese were also ordered to choose between compulsory naturalisation as Vietnamese and evacuation to Formosa. (Those Chinese who had Vietnamese mothers were not allowed to ask for evacuation to Formosa.) Only a handful of Chinese were evacuated, the police confiscated the papers of other Chinese, and there were threats in some districts that those Chinese who had not taken out their new nationality papers by a certain time would be heavily fined.

In Saigon and Cholon the local Chinese rioted in retaliation; Chinese leaders swore that nothing would make them renounce their Chinese nationality. There was a boycott of Vietnamese goods among Chinese merchants in Hong Kong and Singapore; and in a Chinese-organised run on the banks the value of the Vietnamese piastre dropped by about a third on the Hong Kong free market.

Like the Thais the Vietnamese found that the economic restrictions on the Chinese were unenforceable, and there were not enough Vietnamese to take over from the Chinese shopkeepers and traders. At first quietly, and then urged by local officials in the big towns, the Chinese went back to their old trades in 'partnership' with Vietnamese, or working under the names of their Vietnamese wives. But over the new citizenship laws the Chinese gave in and took Vietnamese names and generally Vietnamese papers. The whole appearance of the Chinese suburb of Cholon altered as the Chinese signboards over shops were replaced by Vietnamese signs.

* * *

In the Philippines there were the same difficulties as in Vietnam about finding Filipinos to replace Chinese ousted from the retail trade, but it was less easy than in other south-east Asian countries for Chinese to bribe their way back into their old businesses using Filipino names and 'front men'. In 1959 a new group of Chinese businessmen were threatened when the Philippines Central Bank started to refuse foreign exchange to non-American and non-Filipino firms who wanted to import consumer goods. Chinese, who up to the spring of 1959 had controlled 39 per cent of the Philippines importing business, feared that this was the start of an attempt to force them out of the whole of the Philippines foreign trade.

In Manila it was said that the economic pressure on the Chinese was an attempt of the ministers who followed the popular Ramon Magsaysay to divert Filipino attention from their own economic and political failures; and that the local Chinese would benefit even more than Filipinos from a strong and effective new national leader.

*   *   *

The same desire to divert attention from misgovernment and economic inefficiency was said to account for some of the Indonesian moves against their Chinese community. The local Chinese were particularly useful scapegoats for the Indonesian government. They were unpopular not only with the army, who were afraid of them as potential fifth columnists and communists, but also with most ordinary Indonesians, who believed the current rumours that Indonesian currency troubles, rice shortage and other economic ills were due to the malevolence, greed and hoarding of the Chinese shopkeepers.

It was a nationally popular move when the Indonesian government in 1959 decided to replace Chinese shops in rural areas by Indonesian co-operatives. In west Java the Chinese families involved were told to move into designated areas in the towns, and the Indonesian military governor sent in troops to enforce the new laws. The Chinese alleged that women and children were roughly treated in the forcible evacuation that followed, furniture and homes were wrecked and families were ruined when they had to leave without being given time to sell up their businesses. There were also complaints from all over Indonesia that the new areas allocated for Chinese settlement already had enough shops or were in non-trading areas of the towns. Several thousand Indonesian Chinese families left for China, but not until many of them had been further embittered by ill-treatment at the Indonesian customs posts.

All through the re-settlement and evacuation of the Chinese there was petty official harassing, and among the many protests that Peking made on behalf of the local Chinese, one at least, about their treatment by Borneo officials, must find an echo in the hearts of most travellers to Indonesia. Before the Chinese in Borneo were given exit permits, they had, according to a Peking statement, to have up to 200 fingerprints taken, produce 10 passport-sized photographs, fill up 15 miscellaneous forms, and produce 7 copies of their luggage lists!

It is possible that President Sukarno's government, who had previously enjoyed particularly friendly relations with Peking, were startled by the volume of the Peking protests and the curt treatment given to their foreign minister who was scolded like a schoolboy by the officials of the Chinese foreign office when he visited Peking. The Indonesian embassy to China retorted by issuing a communiqué in which they suggested that the Chinese Communist Party should undertake severe self-criticism. When the Chinese Communist Party defended the Indonesian Chinese, the communiqué said, they were defending petty bourgeois exploiters of the proletariat!

Peking's protests were however forced by the even more strongly worded protests that were being issued by Formosa at the same time. If Peking had not offered the Indonesian Chinese refuge and evacuation ships, Formosa was only too ready to step into her place and make capital from the failure of the communists to shelter even those Chinese who wanted communist citizenship. As it was, Peking's protests to Indonesia were voiced in terms generally more moderate than the Indonesian replies, and considerably more moderate than those China habitually used in the protests she delivered to western powers. Diplomatic relations were not broken off, and there were no overt threats of armed action.

In her dealings with Indonesia China was, however, restrained not only by her desire to avoid trouble and encourage neutralism in south-east Asia generally, but also by the existence of the Indonesian Communist Party. After the Italian party it is the biggest in the non-communist world, its leaders are very able, and the party has been seriously embarrassed by the Indonesian differences with China.

Early in 1960, while the crisis over the rural shop-keepers in Indonesia still continued and after a threatened split in the Indonesian Communist Party, China underlined the continued existence of the Asian United Front by at last agreeing to the formal ratification of her dual-nationality treaty with Indonesia. (Although diplomatic notes still have to be exchanged on how the treaty should be implemented.) The Chinese foreign minister, Chen Yi, said at the ratification ceremony: 'The Chinese government has always been of the opinion that the holding of dual nationality by overseas Chinese is irrational, because this not only runs counter to the vital interests of the overseas Chinese, but also may be made use of by forces hostile to the friendship between our two countries to sow discord and carry out disruptive activities.'

* * *

However, Asian feeling against China was mounting in 1959 and 1960 as there was more news of Chinese oppression in Tibet. There were again openly expressed doubts about whether the loyalties of overseas Chinese could ever be trusted, whether they were ever prepared to live with other Asian peoples as citizens on an equal footing, whether it was Chinese nature to adapt to any political system other than communism or an extreme military dictatorship.

One answer to these doubts will be given by the success or failure of the new government of the mainly Chinese city of Singapore. Since 1959 Singapore has been internally self-governing under the socialist but not communist People's Action Party, led by one of the ablest statesmen in Asia—the young, Cambridge-educated Prime Minister, Lee Kuan-yew. If the People's Action Party government can make a success of the difficult conditions of Singapore they will at least have shown Chinese capacity for democratic government, their ability to compromise with other peoples, and their capacity for loyal work in states outside China.

A major problem facing Lee Kuan-yew in Singapore is that the city and island is not an economically viable unit in itself. One of the aims of the new government therefore has been to encourage the more conservative leadership of the Malayan Federation to accept a merger of Singapore and Malaya. The main obstacle to this merger was that the Chinese of Singapore added to the Chinese of Malaya would mean a Chinese majority in the union, and Malays were afraid that the Chinese would use this majority to tyrannise over them. The Singapore government has tried to show that a Chinese majority need not be tyrannous. Lee Kuan-yew has warned students against 'Chinese chauvinism', a Malay was appointed as the titular head of Singapore, and Singapore officials are encouraged to employ Malay juniors and offer special help to Malay students.

Most Malay and Chinese citizens of Singapore have welcomed the new government's social legislation. There has been a campaign against the gangsters of the Triad Society, pornographic newspapers and books have been suppressed, and some of the more open brothels and the funfairs used as headquarters by pimps and criminals have been shut. This sort of puritan legislation is popular all over Asia. The clean-up in China and the seriousness of Chinese young people has been one of the main attractions of communism to Asians—however drab the new order has appeared to westerners. Most thinking Asians are ashamed of the prostitution, lawlessness and drug-taking in their cities, and non-communist countries like South Vietnam with its camps for reformed prostitutes have imitated some of the aspects of the new Chinese puritanism. But, as yet, Singapore's new legislation is the most sweeping and apparently successful in the region.

Where Lee Kuan-yew has been less successful is in keeping the P.A.P. clear of communist influence. Before the 1959 elections there were allegations that the P.A.P. was communist-dominated and, when the party came to power, some of the suspects previously held by police were immediately released. But Singapore's major laws against communism continued to be enforced, western investment in the colony was encouraged, and Lee Kuan-yew retained many of the colony's previous British officials. But some of the P.A.P.'s leading members are further to the left than Lee himself, and there are signs of growing communist influence in the Singapore municipal government and in the trade unions.

If the P.A.P. government is given time it will benefit from the far better education now being offered to Chinese students in Chinese schools. One of the reasons for the Singapore school riots were the enormous Chinese secondary schools, sometimes with over 5,000 pupils in them, where teachers could not hope to know and influence their individual students. These schools were also privately run, and headmasters were often badgered by management committees of rich men and fund-raisers who were only too ready to interfere in minor questions of timetable arrangements and school discipline.

New government-run Chinese secondary schools with around 1,000 pupils in them have been set up recently, and it is hoped that the better salaries offered in these schools, and the freedom from committee interference will encourage better teachers to work in them.

The main need of these schools, as of Chinese schools everywhere, is for new textbooks. Those of the old ones that are not simply vehicles for communist propaganda are very dull with a heavily Victorian flavour. A standard geography used not only in Singapore but also over much of the rest of south-east Asia consists of the imports and exports of the different provinces of China, the principal rivers and the principal towns and town populations. Nearly all of this information is anyway out of date as the book has not been revised for over ten years. Teachers without strong political views, whose only choice is between this sort of textbook and an up-to-date, if Communist, Peking geography, may be very tempted to choose the brighter, newer Peking text.

Educationally Singapore also houses the unique experiment of Nanyang university, the only university in southeast Asia which offers ordinary university teaching in Chinese. Previously graduates of Chinese secondary schools whose English was below university standards had to go either to the Chinese mainland, or to Formosa, if they wanted higher education. But Nanyang has unfortunately suffered from many of the same difficulties as the Singapore Chinese schools. The university is dependent on private subscriptions, and the salaries offered have not been high enough to attract a sufficient number of good Chinese-speaking university teachers. Non-university members of the board of management have inter-

84

fered in detailed matters of university administration. There has also been political interference both from local communist and from Kuomintang supporters, and in most courses it is even more difficult to get good and non-political Chinese textbooks at the university than at the school level.

During the spring of 1960 the P.A.P. government tried to reform the university administration, and help the raising of Nanyang academic standards to a height that will allow its degrees to be generally recognised.

The success of Nanyang university may decide the future policies of many south-east Asian governments over Chinese schools. It is obvious that Chinese schools which lead only to a university education in China or to discontented school-leavers in south-east Asia who feel that they have been robbed of their chance of further education are dangerous to the countries in which they are working.

Secondary school teachers in Hong Kong, who are themselves refugees from communism, have said that they felt it their duty not to make it impossible for their students to enter Chinese universities: so they deliberately avoided advocating doctrines or teaching facts in their classes which would be dangerous for their pupils to know and discuss in China. Yet a purely restrictive policy like Thailand's which aims at closing as many Chinese schools as possible without providing adequate alternative education naturally embitters Chinese parents. Where good alternative schools are provided, however, many Chinese parents prefer them to purely Chinese schools. Over much of south-east Asia wealthy parents already send their children to mission schools because they believe that an English-language education offers them a better start in life than a Chinese-language education would. Similarly the popularity of Dutch-Chinese schools and the Malay-Chinese schools among the

Indonesian Chinese suggests that schools in south-east Asian countries which offered optional classes in Chinese culture and a Chinese language, together with teaching in the local language and perhaps a European language, would probably be preferred to purely Chinese schools.

10

Repression or assimilation?

JUST how repressive south-east Asian countries should
be in any aspect of their policy towards their Chinese
minorities is something each country must decide for
itself in the light of local conditions. Ideally it is obvious
that a positive policy—building new primary schools on
the old Indonesian Malay-Chinese pattern or better
secondary schools as the Singapore government is doing,
rather than simply closing existing unsatisfactory ones—
is likely to produce more loyal Chinese citizens for the
country concerned. But many south-east Asian governments would answer that they have neither the money
nor the trained teachers to build these new schools, and
Thailand, which has closed most of its Chinese schools,
also has a high proportion of assimilated Chinese.

Even if south-east Asian governments cannot afford
numbers of new schools they might consider it worth
while to inspect existing Chinese schools, ban certain of
the most undesirable textbooks, and enforce minimum
standards on teachers, including perhaps ability to read
and write the local language. New textbooks to replace
those banned may have to be specially commissioned.
But conscientious teachers will be unwilling to use new
texts that are simply propaganda for the governments
concerned, nor are textbooks of that sort likely to appeal
to children. But textbook writers could legitimately encourage the child's pride in the country he was born in
and emphasise the duty he owes to the people among
whom he lives. Properly written, these textbooks should
be more interesting to children and easier to teach from

than anything written in China. The local writer has the advantage of being able to draw examples from the country the children know, and show them how the south-east Asian society they live in is related to the past and to the geographical background of the familiar countryside.

Most Chinese schools will wish to teach their pupils something of China's history and culture, and this again could be illustrated by examples of Chinese influence and trade with the south-east Asian countries concerned, and placed against a general world background. In the end good new textbooks, interweaving Chinese and local culture, may greatly enrich south-east Asia and give all children there, whatever their racial origin, the benefit of the best in two civilisations.

With foreign-subsidised Chinese newspapers, as with schools, a firm policy offers certain easy advantages. The Indonesian restrictions on Chinese newspapers include as conditions of publication that 60 per cent of news space must be given to reporting on Indonesia, and newspapers must print lessons in the Indonesian language for their Chinese readers. But the difficulty has been to enforce these restrictions, and there is the same difficulty of practical enforcement about any attempt to prevent communist and nationalist subsidies being paid to south-east Asian newspapers.

What does seem to defeat its purpose is a general Press slanting of news from China, or a complete censorship on all Chinese news. Very few Chinese, whatever Taiwan propagandists may like to think, are going to believe that China today is starving or powerless. Local Chinese communities often still have strong ties with China, and their own ways of getting some news. One of the effects of obvious anti-communist propaganda is to make them particularly ready to believe counter-propaganda from Peking.

Another effect of obvious lying is to make visitors to China believe what their Intourist guides tell them, because they see around them evidence of material advancement, cleanliness and honesty for which they were not prepared. On the other hand if south-east Asian countries genuinely believe that they can offer their people— Chinese and local—a better life than communism has given to mainland China they have everything to gain from honest reporting. Overseas Chinese communities have already shown their repugnance to some of the work of the communists—particularly the purge of the landlords and the social changes caused by the communes.

About the nationalisation of Chinese in south-east Asian countries, some degree of compulsion or, at least, forceful persuasion seems in practice to have paid. In spite of the exhortations of Chou En-lai only a minority of the Chinese in Burma have become Burmese citizens— perhaps because there was no official discrimination against local Chinese who continued to hold Chinese citizenship. In South Vietnam, on the other hand, compulsory Vietnamese citizenship for the Chinese worked, at any rate on paper; and in Thailand where there was less compulsion, but obvious economic and social advantages, in becoming a Thai citizen the majority of second- and third-generation Chinese have become Thais. Their difficulty however is that China does not recognise their Thai status, and other Thais are today naturally suspicious of fellow-citizens whose loyalty is claimed by another nation, and who can appeal to that nation for protection.

Thailand, like the other south-east Asian countries, is watching to see how the Sino-Indonesian dual-nationality treaty will work out in practice; and what will be the effect of the Indonesian government's present drastic restrictions on those who remain Chinese. The unfairness many Chinese have complained of in the Indonesian government's measures is that the restrictions, particularly those on the rural traders, were too sweeping; that they were imposed before the dual-nationality treaty was ratified and Chinese enabled to become Indonesian citizens under it; and thirdly that the restrictions were combined with general anti-Chinese feeling and statements, particularly from Indonesian army leaders, aimed both at those Chinese who wanted to become good Indonesian citizens and those whose loyalties lay outside Indonesia.

Entirely repressive policies aimed indiscriminately at all members of an overseas Chinese community do not seem to work well. If large numbers of Chinese are driven out of south-east Asian countries, or refuse to co-operate in any way with the governments there, the economies of the region are liable to be very badly damaged—as South Vietnam's was after the attempt to get Chinese out of the rice trade; and Indonesia's when the rural Chinese traders were evicted. Most villagers in Indonesia are now faced with rising prices and sometimes closed shops. In one area of west Java there were only 200 Indonesian co-operatives ready but the Chinese had to leave 2,500 scattered shops. In general all over south-east Asia there are not enough local shopkeepers, artisans and merchants to replace the local Chinese. Moreover those Chinese who remained in south-east Asian countries, in spite of repressive policies aimed at them, would become an embittered minority, turned in on themselves, and conscious of enmity and strangers all round them.

In the future other south-east Asian countries may find that a balanced policy towards the Chinese in their country pays them best. Some restrictions on non-citizens and their rights to work and trade are common to most countries in the west as well as in Asia. But anywhere in the world compulsory citizenship or economic restrictions which ruin non-citizens make for a very flimsy sort of assimilation. A compulsory citizen may also be a very embittered citizen unless he has been trained in loyalty to his new country through schools and newspapers; and this loyalty to his new country will come more easily to him if he is not torn too much between its claims and those of his motherland.

Future Chinese claims on particular overseas Chinese communities, and Chinese willingness to negotiate citizenship treaties with south-east Asian countries, depend partly on those countries' individual relations with China, and partly on China's views about Asian and world politics. The diplomatic recognition of China by those countries who have not already done so is an obvious step towards general relaxation of Asian political tension; diplomatic recognition from the SEATO countries would also probably reduce Chinese fears that Formosa might be used as a base against her, and reduce the volume of the protests Peking feels called on to make on behalf of Chinese citizens and Chinese claims.

One difficulty however about other attempts to relax tension in Asia is that apparently Chinese officials in charge of foreign affairs know very little about the outside world. They do not understand what other Asians think about overseas Chinese communities, or indeed about the actions of China herself. The most startling recent example was the apparent Chinese surprise at the unpopularity of Chou En-lai with Indian crowds when he visited India after Tibet and the Indian border crisis.

There are also other possible explanations of the startling tactlessness of Chinese officials when they contradict all talk of the United Front in Asia by, for instance, keeping waiting the ambassadors of neutral nations who are trying to deliver important notes. One explanation is the old Chinese dislike of foreigners and indifference to what goes on outside her own borders. Another is the possible conflict in Chinese foreign policy between the pragmatists (who are also the internationalists and the generally more liberal and friendly section of the party) led by Chou En-lai against the narrow, entirely Marxist, and very ignorant 'China-firsters' led possibly by Liu Shao-chi.

Whatever explanation, or combination of explanations, is true, south-east Asian countries could, if they recognised China, play some part in correcting ignorance or strengthening the position of the potentially friendly party. Embassies could explain their country's points of view over problems like that of the overseas Chinese; and for every south-east Asian delegation invited to China, a Chinese delegation could be invited back and on tours of the countries see something of what conditions in non-communist Asia are really like.

But Chinese ignorance of the outside world and Chinese xenophobia would be far more shaken by admission to the United Nations and its subsidiary bodies, and by tours of the larger nations outside Asia. South-east Asia will find the solution to all its problems of relations with China, including that of the overseas Chinese, easier when general world relations with China are easier and founded on better knowledge on both sides. But meanwhile Asian governments who both fear and benefit from their overseas Chinese communities can themselves at least decide which of their fears are justifiable and which unjustifiable, and do something to increase the benefits their countries gain from their latest immigrants.

Suggestions for further reading:

BRIMMELL, J. H. *Communism in South East Asia.* Oxford University Press. 1959.

FRIED, MORTON H., Edit. *Colloquium on the Overseas Chinese.* International Secretariat of the Institute of Pacific Relations. 1958.

HALL, D. G. E. *A History of South-East Asia.* Macmillan. 1955.

KAHIN, GEORGE McT., Edit. *Governments and Politics of Southeast Asia.* Cornell University Press. 1959.

PURCELL, VICTOR. *The Chinese in Southeast Asia.* Oxford University Press. 1951. (The most detailed and authoritative study.)

PURCELL, VICTOR. *The Chinese in Malaya.* Oxford University Press. 1948.

PYE, LUCIEN W. *Guerilla Communism in Malaya. Its Social and Political Meaning.* Princeton University Press. 1956.

SKINNER, WILLIAM G. *Chinese Society in Thailand.* Cornell University Press. 1957. (A particularly useful study of the Chinese community and its changing relations with the Thai people and government.)

SKINNER, WILLIAM G. *Leadership and Power in the Chinese Community of Thailand.* Cornell University Press. 1958.

THOMPSON, VIRGINIA and ADLOFF, RICHARD. *Minority Problems in Southeast Asia.* Stanford University Press. 1955.